Psychic Power

Dragonhawk Publishing Titles

General
Treasures of the Unicorn
More Simplified Magic
The Animal-Wise Tarot
Animal-Wise

Beginnings: A Dragonhawk Series
Music Therapy for Non-Musicians
Psychic Protection

Young Person's School of Magic and Mystery
Magic of Believing
Psychic Power

FORTHCOMING:

Dreamtime Magic
Star Magic
Spirits, Ghosts, and Guardians
Faerie Charms
Healing Arts
Divination and Scrying
Word Magic
Ancient Powers

Young Person's School of Magic and Mystery

VOLUME II:

Psychic Power

by

Ted Andrews

DRAGONHAWK PUBLISHING   JACKSON, TENNESSEE

A DRAGONHAWK PUBLISHING BOOK

Psychic Power

(Volume II of *Young Person's School of Magic and Mystery*)
Text and cover copyright ©2000 by Ted Andrews

First Edition

ISBN 1-888767-40-5

Library of Congress Catalog Card Number: 00-100045

This book was designed and produced by

Dragonhawk Publishing
Jackson, Tennessee
USA

Dedication

For my ESP Club at
Ankeney Junior High and
all of my students

Table of Contents

Table of Contents (CONT.)

Magical Practices
(Exercises)

Magical Practices (cont.)
(Exercises)

Preface
A Word to Parents and Students

The world truly is a place of great magic, mystery, and wonder. No group of people is more aware of this than our children. They know the rustling of leaves is a kind of whisper and wishing upon a star has great power. They know there really are ghosts and spirits and that their dreams are glimpses into other worlds and possibilities.

Young people have a great interest in the mystical, the psychic, and the magical, but much of what they know has come to them distorted by movies and television or complicated through confusing books that often are written in clouded, adult "New Age-speak." Too often the psychic and magical world becomes a place of fear and doubts rather than a place of wonder and enchantment. Without meeting their unique learning needs and skill levels, or without the right guidance and encouragement, the magic in the child disappears.

From preschoolers to teenagers and college students, interest in the psychic, the spiritual, and the magical is exploding. Parents are more aware than ever that their children are seeing auras, speaking of past lives, and experiencing spirit. Many of our young people are demonstrating healing touch or having prophetic dreams. And yet little has ever been created to encourage this interest or to help develop these skills within the young. What is most often missing is a way of helping them understand and work with their magical abilities and intuitive energies.

Although there has always been a great deal of material available for general development of psychic abilities, most of the materials and techniques are not designed to meet the unique needs of young people. Generally what has been written is for adults, and while some of it may be applicable to young people, a great deal of the material is not suitable for them (and sometimes not even for the adults themselves). Determining what is suitable can be difficult for those who are experienced. For the young and inexperienced, it is nearly impossible.

The creation of the YOUNG PERSON'S SCHOOL OF MAGIC AND MYSTERY resolves this problem. Great care has been taken to develop a unique course of study which can be beneficial and enjoyable for the young person wishing to unfold his or her own inner magic. It will also benefit the inexperienced and young-at-heart adult explorer as well.

To make this even more possible, we have gathered a faculty of delightful and skilled teachers to develop this course of study to guide the young seeker into new realms of possibilities. All are extremely knowledgeable and experienced in teaching both the young and adults. They are experts in their areas of study, and they can demonstrate all they teach. They live the magical life.

As we began to look more closely at all of them, we found they have other unique qualities in common. All of our teachers are well rounded in their education and experience. They are all practical and grounded, and they have a contagious enthusiasm about their work and their life. And most importantly, they have both a sense of responsibility and a sense of humor about themselves, about the world, and especially about the magical life.

Our teachers provide techniques which are safe and productive. Their methods, exercises, and games are intended to develop, entertain, and affirm the magic that exists in us all. Each course in the school supports and adds to what comes before or follows. Through this study, young people who feel "different" will become more accepting of their unique gifts. Their inner gifts will blossom throughout life and the creative contributions of these young people to the adult world in the new millenium will go well beyond what we can imagine!

We have chosen an initial ten subjects, although others will be added in time. We believe these provide a strong foundation for the student and will lay the groundwork for future, in-depth magical development. However, we will not be learning about casting spells or turning enemies into toads. This school is about helping young people find their inner magic and developing it over a lifetime.

If you provide the right teachers with the right methods, the magic will unfold. While many of us as children had to ignore, fear, or hide our special experiences, today's young people can now embrace and understand these happenings. Their experiences can become invitations to a life of great magic and wonder.

For parents, the YOUNG PERSON'S SCHOOL OF MAGIC AND MYSTERY provides a wonderful opportunity to explore spiritual mysteries with their children. This series provides guidance for working effectively with young people exploring what adults were often never encouraged as children to explore themselves. For young people, this series will keep their dreams, their wonders, and their awareness of the possibilities of life forever strong.

We strongly encourage parents to share the experiences and explorations in the exercises with the young people in their lives. Together, we can all nurture and guide each other into new realms of wonder.

Dragonhawk Publishing

Young Person's School of Magic and Mystery

A Complete Course of Study in Ten Volumes

The Magic of Believing
Psychic Power
Dreamtime Magic
Spirits, Ghosts, and Guardians
Faerie Charms
Star Magic
Healing Arts
Divination and Scrying
Word Magic
Ancient Powers

Lesson 1

The World of Psychic Powers

Have you ever had a hunch come true?

Have you ever known who was phoning
before answering the ring?

Have you known what others were going to say
before they said it?

Have you ever had a feeling about something
and have it come true

Have you ever thought about a person and
have them call or show up at the door?

Have you ever decided to make an
unscheduled stop and then benefit from it?

Have you been able to sense another person's mood
before you even speak to them?

Have you known whether you liked or disliked
someone the moment you met the person?

Auras. ESP. Ghosts and spirits. Telepathy. Visions of the future. Astral travel. Prophetic dreams.

The psychic world is filled with unusual words for mysterious experiences, words that intrigue us, words that stir a deep part of us. The truth is these experiences are often quite normal, but there is a great deal of misunderstanding about them.

All of us at some point in our lives will have some kind of psychic experience. A hunch will prove itself true. We may have a dream about something that will happen. We feel uncomfortable about a person or place and our feeling turns out to be accurate. We may even see the spirit of a special person in our lives who has passed on. Remember, when something happens we can't explain, our inability to understand what went on doesn't mean it wasn't real. We just don't see the whole picture yet.

I have always been able to see and know things others have seemed not to notice. For the most part, I have enjoyed and appreciated this. I almost always knew when there was a surprise test coming in school. I have grandparents who bring me messages from the spirit world. Animals speak to me. Nature spirits show themselves to me. When I was teaching school, I watched the auras of my students so I could tell when something was amiss. I can usually see or feel the health problems of people around me.

Yet there have been times I have also hated this ability. I have forseen the death of my father and some of my friends. I am sensitive to environments around me. I very easily "pick up" on the energy of places and the events surrounding them and this can affect my emotions and moods. I have had feelings, impressions, and even spirit become intrusive and bothersome at times. I know when people are thinking negatively of me and when people may not be as trustworthy as they appear.

Imagine if...

You could *really* know things through your psychic ability and intuition. How would your life be different if you could...

- sense trouble around you,

- know a test or quiz was coming,

- tell what someone really thought about you,

- see what some people are truly like when you first meet them,

- send thoughts to another person instead of passing notes in school,

- pick up on other people's true moods,

- detect when someone is lying,

- know if someone really likes you,

- feel how healthy a person is,

- sense when a person is thinking about you,

- see fairies, elves, and nature spirits,

- sense people special to you who have died, or even see them,

- watch your dreams come true,

- see angels, and

- foresee the future.

Imagine the possibilities!

Psychic Absurdicus

Fun, Absurd, and Strange
Psychic Practices

HOW TO KNOW
THE FUTURE

Take the stone which is called Benam which is like a Beastes tooth, and put it under thy tongue. And as Aaron and the old philosophers say, as long as thou dost hold it there, thou mayest conjecture and tell of things to come. And thou shalt not erre in any wise for judging.

Albertus Magnus,
Magical Stones

Of course, with a stone beneath your tongue, your speech would be quite garbled and not likely to be understood. How would we know then whether the "conjecture" were true or false?

Because of this, I have had to learn to become cautious and protective of my energies and myself.

Just the same, my abilities to pick up on subtle things around me are not unique. I am no more special or gifted than anyone else. Actually, there are more people like me than different. Most people, thought, try to ignore these feelings and experiences. Adults, especially, don't believe it when others report these kinds of experiences. Often people become frightened because they do not understand what is happening.

I believe the only difference between myself and others is that as a child I could be quite stubborn (well, yes, as an adult too, but just not quite as obnoxiously stubborn). Even as a child, no one was going to make me believe what I experienced wasn't real. I have always tried to understand and control these strange, psychic experiences instead of ignoring them.

All of this psychic stuff is actually quite simple and not as complicated or mysterious as many would have you believe. We now know more about the mind and its capabilities than ever before, and as you go through this book, you will become more and more aware of just how powerful you really are, how your own psychic abilities are far greater than you ever imagined.

We All Have Hunches

Hunches, or impressions, are the simplest kinds of psychic experiences. They are instinctive, much in the way animals respond to the world around them. Animals actively sense whether someone is kind, whether a place is safe, and whether they can relax or need to become protective, depending upon what they find.

Usually hunches are the first things to affect us. They are vague feelings we often cannot explain. When we

Psych Out

A lady once asked Thomas Edison,
"What is electricity?"

His answer was,
"Madam, electricity is—use it."

This is good advice for us as well.
Psychic power is—just use it!

walk into a new place or meet someone new, do we feel comfortable or uncomfortable? Easy or uneasy? Does the place or the person feel warm, safe, and trustworthy? Your first impressions are often correct. A part of our instinctual nature watches out for us, automatically "sensing" our environment. It's part of our intuition, and like an internal radar system, scans everything around us.

When we enter a new environment, this instinctual part of us awakens and immediately begins to sense what's around us. This intuitive sense keeps us alert and open to subtle changes. In everyday settings, most people ignore it. In new places, this sense generally becomes more acute and we notice the message. Have you ever been told when you were uncomfortable in a new place, "It's only because it's new" or "You're just not used to everything yet." Our impressions at these times are often very accurate. Unfortunately, we are generally not taught how to recognize this intuitive radar and understand its messages, much less how to develop this ability and be able to use it at any time.

Psychic comes from the word "psyche," meaning *soul*, that creative part of you that instinctively watches out for you. It is the source of your hunches and impressions. It is your Inner Guardian, recognizing patterns and perceiving subtle things, alerting, warning, protecting, and enlightening you. It is your creative and instinctual part and everyone has these abilities.

Myths About Psychic Power

Now that you know we all have psychic abilities, it's helpful to look at the three main myths about psychic power.

Myth 1:

ONLY A FEW SPECIAL PEOPLE ARE ACTUALLY PSYCHIC.

Psychic power is an ability EVERYONE has. We can all learn to develop and employ it within our lives. Some individuals may be able to develop this ability more easily than others, but remember, psychic sensitivity is like any learned skill. It takes time and practice.

I spent seven years as a reading specialist in the public school system. One of the things I learned is that anyone can learn to read. Some may pick reading up more easily than others, but EVERYONE can learn to do it. Even if people only learn to read on a functional level, they enhance their lives tremendously, opening themselves up to up greater opportunities.

Psychic skills vary among people in much the same way. Some are able to pick the skill up more easily than others, but EVERYONE can learn it. Even if people learn to become only slightly skilled in their use of their psychic abilities, their lives are tremendously empowered.

I know people who have a lot more native psychic ability than I do, people who could probably develop their skills more easily than I have mine, possibly even expressing those skills in ways I would be unable to. However, I have worked to develop my skills, surpassing the abilities of some of those with greater natural talent. And I practice my psychic skills frequently so they don't get rusty.

Many people believe psychic or spiritual activities are only for the gifted, a "special few." When we assume others are more special than we are, we are giving away our own power. We are lowering our self-esteem. We are setting ourselves up for failure and dependence upon others. Instead of creating our own light, we are limiting and blocking our own natural abilities, whether these be psychic or any other creative talents.

Remember, you can do anything anyone else is doing. All you have to do is persist and find the way that works best for you.

MYTH 2:

WE CANNOT CONTROL PSYCHIC EXPERIENCES.

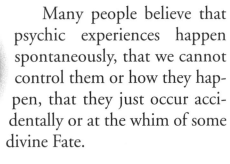

Many people believe that psychic experiences happen spontaneously, that we cannot control them or how they happen, that they just occur accidentally or at the whim of some divine Fate.

BUT THIS IS NOT SO.

Our lives are not up to Fate. We have free will and tremendous creative abilities, including psychic sensitivities. These potentials are within each of us and we can develop and control how they are expressed.

Others believe that psychic experiences happen because of some unusual and often traumatic circumstances in life. How often have you heard stories or seen movies in which an individual becomes psychic after a horrible accident? These kinds of books and movies imply that the reward for going through hell is some kind of special, psychic power.

BUT THIS IS ALSO NOT SO.

These are just books. These are just movies. They make good stories, but these kinds of happenings are extremely rare in real life, although they do occur once in a while. Unfortunately, the people who have these kinds of psychic awakenings usually are unable to control their experiences. Often they can't tell whether the psychic perceptions are real or just illusions.

We do not have to traumatize ourselves in order to awaken our psychic power. Nor is it up to the Fates as to when we have our psychic experiences. We can develop and control our psychic powers to a tremendous degree no matter what age and no matter what we have or have not done in life. We can learn to turn psychic abilities on and off at will—whenever and wherever we want!

Myth 3:

WE MUST STAY TUNED IN ALL OF THE TIME OR
WE WILL LOSE OUR PSYCHIC ABILITY.

Over the years I have been amazed at how often I have heard statements like "I'll lose my ability if I don't stay tuned in," or "what if I can't turn my abilities back on again if I turn them off?" I have even met a great number of professionals in the field who believe this. In truth, these ideas are based on superstition and fear and have nothing to do with reality.

Those who are afraid of "tuning out" believe on some level that they have been given something special and if they turn it off, they may not be able to get it back again. They apparently believe their psychic power is just a fluke or a whim of Fate. As quickly as it arose, it could also disappear. They have either forgotten or don't realize psychic ability is a learned skill.

Often, psychics who try to stay tuned in all the time will have some very obvious problems. You can usually recognize them. They drain themselves physically, emotionally, mentally, and spiritually. It shows. They tire more and more easily. They will usually look and feel much older than their years, often worn out and haggard. They appear as if they have been put through a wringer and have little vitality about them.

Living tuned in all the time leads to a variety of health problems for people of this mindset. When illness hits, they will usually take longer to recover and be more likely to develop complications. They are often susceptible to depression and mood swings.

On the other hand, those who learn to control their psychic abilities and turn them on and off at will are also easily recognized. They have a great energy about them no matter what their age and often look and feel younger than they are. They are increasingly creative in all they do. They actually seem to shine. When they do get ill, they recover quickly. And they are usually exuberant about life.

Benefits of Psychic Power

Everyone's skills are different and everyone's speed of psychic development varies, but EVERYONE can develop and learn to use their abilities. You are already psychic. All you need to do is awaken these abilities and practice, practice, practice them!

People work to develop their psychic power for a variety of reasons. Some want to be able to know when trouble is coming. Some want to know when tests and quizzes will pop up in school. Some want to be able to tell when others are lying or being deceitful—especially if there's a boyfriend or girlfriend involved. Some want help in finding their true love. Others want to know the future. There are almost as many reasons for developing our psychic abilities as there are people wanting to do so.

Regardless of our personal reasons for developing our psychic skills, the benefits are many. Awakening our psychic abilities helps us:

➤ become self-empowered,

realizing we are more capable in life than we may have imagined

➤ make more appropriate choices in life,

bettering our chances of making good decisions

➤ sense more easily how others are responding to us,

developing stronger, more effective relationships

➤ avoid problems,

> *foreseeing possible problems and before they become major difficulties*

➤ become better judges of character,

> *gaining insight into old and new relationships*

➤ see more clearly in times of emergency, and

➤ become more creative and successful in all we do.

Once we learn to awaken our psychic abilities properly, we can always do so again, no matter how long we have ignored them or skipped practicing them.

How many of you can ride a bike? Do you think you will ever forget how? What if you didn't ride that bike for a couple of years? Do you think you could still ride it? Of course you could. You might be a little out of practice, but you would still be able to ride the bike. And the same is true of psychic ability.

Psychic ability is a potential within each of us. Once again, let me emphasize that it is not a gift for the special few. It is a tool available to each one of us. Whether we develop our psychic abililty is entirely up to each one of us. Everyone can learn to turn their psychic ability on and off at will and to use it as needed.

And that is what we will learn throughout the rest of this book.

Magical Practice

Creating Your Sacred Space

skills developed
- creates a place to go within to your inner self
- strengthens ability to tap into psychic senses

One of the keys to learning to shift to our magical and psychic self at will is to create a sacred space. Sacred spaces shift our attention and focus from the normal daily activities to magical ones. They help us to hear our inner voice more clearly. MOST PSYCHIC EXPERIENCES HAVE TO DO WITH LISTENING TO THE INNER SELF.

If you have ever been some place where you felt a great sense of peace, you have experienced a sacred place. If you have ever been so relaxed and into some activity that you lost track of time, you have experienced a sense of sacred space. There is a shift away from "normal" thinking and feeling. Sometimes this experience is referred to as an altered state of consciousness. This just means that our focus has shifted. The trick is to be able to get yourself to this sacred space whenever you want to go there.

The Purpose of the Sacred Place

Sacred spaces provide powerful magical intersections in our lives where our inner and outer worlds meet. They are places and times—intersections—where the physical and spiritual can come together. Where the past, present, and future flow together to help us understand how each affects the other. Where psychic perceptions become stronger and more normal. Through sacred spaces, the veils separating worlds and creative wonders become the most thin.

To awaken and develop your psychic power, you need to create a sacred space, a place where you can go for all of your psychic and magical explorations. This will be an actual place in the outer world that connects you to your inner world of magical abilities. It can be as simple as the corner of your room. You should have space enough to sit and you should be able to shut out distractions

How to Create Your Own Sacred Space

In Volume I of this series, *Magic of Believing,* we did an exercise called "Castle's Keep." It is a wonderful place,

Magical Practice

Guidelines for Creating

➤ **You do not need a large space.**

A corner of a room where you can spend a half hour or so undisturbed and quiet is all that is necessary.

➤ **Create an altar or sacred center.**

This can be a desktop that is cleared or a fold-out table. It does not need to be large. Use the table to set special items on that help you shift your awareness from the outer world to your inner world.

➤ **Make the time special with clothing and preparations just for your sacred space.**

Use a meditation or prayer shawl (a special blanket, towel, or cloth used only for this). Each time you use it in your magical practices or have it with you, you charge it with magical energy. Eventually, all you will have to do is wrap it around you, pull it up over the head, or even just sit on it, and it begins to shift you from normal everyday type of thinking to your creative, psychic, and magical part.

I have several meditation cloths that I sit on or drape about my shoulders and head. One I use for healing and the other one is just for meditation. I also have a special meditation rug about two feet by three feet—my magic carpet. I unfold it and sit upon it in all my meditations.

Creating Sacred Space (cont.)

Your Own Sacred Space

➤ **Have a special cloth you use only for your magical work.**

This is sometimes called an altar cloth. It should cover part of the surface or easily spread out before you. You can set items on it that are helpful and special to you.

➤ **Have aids to help you.**

Candles, incense, or whatever is comfortable and special for you are wonderful aids to creating sacred space.

➤ **Create a portable sacred space if necessary.**

Your portable sacred space can be as simple as a candle and a cloth you take with you. I do a lot of work outdoors, so I have a box of sacred things that I can carry around with me. If you can leave your items out in your space without their being disturbed, do so. Then all you need do to activate the sacred energy is light a candle. However, if you share a room with others, you may need to keep your sacred space portable. The packing up and unpacking of your magical things provides good preparation and help create your shift to your magical self.

Magical Practice

an inner sacred space for exploring psychic abilities, linking us to our outer sacred space, the place where we perform our meditations and magical practices.

One of the turrets in my castle is very high, and from it I can see in all directions for miles and miles. I use this turret in meditation to "see things," whether it's those things coming my way or those things behind me and how the events of the past have shaped where I am now.

I have used the following techniques to make my turret into a sacred space:

➤ by placing it away from the rest of the castle (all of the everyday things),

➤ by keeping it quiet and peaceful, allowing for less distractions,

➤ by providing a great view so I can get a perspective on problems and events going in and out of my life, and

➤ by connecting it to a sacred space in my everyday world.

When I create a sacred space in my home, it becomes a doorway to my castle and the sacred places within it. It is a place away from the rest of the house, quiet and peaceful. When I meditate there, I can get a handle on troubles and a better perspective of things.

Creating Sacred Space (cont.)

Sacred spaces can be anywhere and any time. However, it is up to you to make them sacred and special. You are the one who needs to create your own bridge between worlds and to new possibilities.

Opening and Closing the Sacred Doors

Having a place and time where we can get in touch with our inner abilities is very important. It helps us learn to use our magical and psychic abilities whenever we need them. Creating sacred space sets up a time and place to tap into our magic self. It changes the atmosphere of the room around you.

The atmosphere around you becomes softer, calmer, and more peaceful. This is the magical shift from the outer to the inner. Close your eyes and just enjoy the sacred space. Throughout the rest of this volume we will learn to use this sacred space to awaken and bring out our psychic power and other magical abilities.

Make sure you will not be disturbed.

Having a time and place where you will not be interrupted or disturbed is most important in creating your sacred space. This includes making sure that phones don't ring in the midst of your magical work and that others do not intrude and disturb you. Remember that this is a sacred and special time for you.

Magical Practice

When I was growing up, I shared my bedroom with three of my brothers. Many of you may be sharing a room with others just as I was when I was growing up. Not exactly conducive to sacred spaces. The primary goals of my brothers and me were to torment each other and bother each other as much as possible. We were constantly getting into each other's stuff.

If you share your room with others, it may take a little more planning to create your sacred space and find your special time to practice without being disturbed. Talk with your brothers and sisters about having times to be left alone. Talk with your parents about helping to get others in the household to respect and honor your times. It may take some extra effort to create your sacred times and space, but in the end, it will be worth it.

SET THE MOOD WITH CANDLES, INCENSE, AND EVEN MUSIC.

Set up your altar area if you are using one. Lay out all of your special items. Include your altar cloth, candles, and anything else that is special or sacred to you. It sets the mood.

The lighting of the candles and putting them out will signal the opening and closing of your sacred doors. The lighting of the candles signals the awakening of your magical self and your sacred space. Putting the candles out signals the closing of your sacred space.

Creating Sacred Space (cont.)

If you use music, keep it soft and unintrusive. The volume should be low and the music what you find relaxing. It should not interfere with your concentration. Do not use radio music, as the shifting from one song rhythm to another and from commercial to commercial can be disrupting.

When you have set up your sacred space, light your candle (you may wish to use more than one) and take a seated position. There are those who claim you need to mark the space more magically, but for our purposes, nothing more is needed than what I've mentioned here.

USE A RELAXATION TECHNIQUE TO CALM
YOURSELF AND GO WITHIN.

Relaxation is important to the success of all magical and psychic practices. There are two kinds of relaxation techniques that are good to master. You will find them beneficial in all of your magical practices throughout this series.

PROGRESSIVE RELAXATION:

Make yourself comfortable and take a few slow, deep breaths. Send warm, soothing thoughts and energy to every part of your body.

Start with your feet and move slowly up to the top of your head. Take your time . The more relaxed you are, the easier it is to bring out your Inner Guardian.

Magical Practice

RHYTHMIC BREATHING:

Begin slow, rhythmic breathing. Breathe naturally, but slowly. Inhale slowly through the nostrils for a count of four to five. Hold your breath for a count of four and then exhale slowly for a count of four to five.

Imagine and feel warm soothing energy flowing to every part of your body with every breath you take. Breathe deeply, relaxing. Focus on being as comfortable and as relaxed as possible.

Always close your sacred doors behind you when you are finished and leave your sacred space.

It is important to close down our sacred times and become *grounded*. Our focus should always be on our daily lives. We use sacred space to bring out our inner abilities, but only so we can use them more effectively in our normal activities.

When we create and use sacred space, we experience what is called an *altered state*. We change our normal way of feeling and thinking to get past the limitations and walls or daily living. However, we always need to re-connect with the physical world.

We close the doors behind us by extinguishing the candles and returning our focus to our regular life. Grounding yourself after your magical practices helps with this.

Creating Sacred Space (cont.)

Grounding is also a way of anchoring the energy of the exercise into your outer life. It is also a way of getting rid of the spacey, disconnected feeling that sometimes occurs with meditation.

So after any meditation, stretch a little. Eat a few crackers or something light. It will help the body focus on digestion.

If you are keeping a Book of Enchantment or journal, write down your experiences from the magical practice. Also offer some vocal form of appreciation and gratitude. It can be a prayer or affirmation.

So far we've described how to create your sacred space and told you about the kinds of things you need to do before and after you make your visit. The table on the following two pages summarize these preparations so they can be reviewed quickly and easily.

As you get used to visiting your sacred space, you will find that your efforts to set the mood, relax, and ground yourself will become second nature to you and you won't have to think about them so much.

Magical Practice

Beginning and Ending Your

Set the Mood (preparing for the exercise)

Begin a magical practice by finding a time to be by yourself when you will not be disturbed or interrupted. You may wish to set the tone by using candles or fragrances.

Relaxation (beginning the exercise)

There are two kinds of relaxation techniques used to begin the exercises. Use the method that works best for you.

progressive relaxation

Make yourself comfortable. Take a few slow, deep breaths and send warm, soothing thoughts to every part of your body, starting with your feet and moving to the top of your head. Visualize warm, soothing energy melting up over you from your feet to your head. Take your time with this. The more relaxed you are, the more quickly and easily you will succeed.

rhythmic breathing

Inhale slowly through the nostrils, hold the breath, and then exhale slowly through the mouth. Imagine warm, soothing energy flowing to every part of your body. As you relax, allow your attention to be focused entirely upon yourself.

Creating Sacred Space (cont.)

Magical Practices (exercises)

Grounding Ritual (ending the exercise)

Altered states tend to draw us away from the physical, so after our magical practices, we need to ground, to reconnect with the physical world.

Grounding should always involve a little stretching. Eating a few crackers is also helpful. By eating something light, the body begins to focus on digestion, which also helps ground us.

Writing in your Book of Enchantment about your feelings and observations after an exercise also grounds those energies into the physical.

The grounding should also involve some vocal expression of affirmation and gratitude. This can be a prayer of thanks for what already is.

Magical Practice

Listening to Your Inner Guardian

skills developed
- **helps in relaxing**
- **strengthens perceptions**
- **improves ability to recognize your psychic self**

Within you is someone of great potential and great wisdom. Within you is someone who is growing and developing great magical abilities and wonders. Within you is the Inner Guardian. The Inner Guardian takes many forms. It's a part of your, the spiritual and magical part of you that links you to the Divine and to your most creative abilities.

Your Inner Guardian might be a *you* that you haven't quite recognized yet, but working with Volumes I and II of this series, you know you are unfolding possibilities for yourself that you never before imagined!

Your Inner Guardian is your magical self, sometimes called your Higher Self or your creative spark. In Volume I, *Magic of Believing*, you first met your Inner Guardian in the magical practice, "Creating the Magical Body." Most people keep their Inner Guardian tucked away, deep inside themselves. But with every expression of your own inner magic, with every potential and possibility you develop, your Inner Guardian becomes stronger and more powerful in your daily life.

Your Inner Guardian is the new, more conscious you, the more ideal you, the brightest and most creative part of you. Your Inner Guardian is your inner spiritual companion that guides and guards you if you allow it to. Although people talk about their Higher Self as if it is a separate entity, it really isn't. It's a seed within you, just waiting to sprout and grow.

In this exercise, you will begin to look upon this wise guardian as someone who is an image of the ideal you, the part of you who sees and knows all. Through this exercise, you will learn to listen to your Inner Guardian's wise voice. In the beginning, we must create a sacred space to invite this part of ourselves out of our mind's closet into the open. However, in time—and with practice—your Inner Guardian will no longer be hidden or hard to find. Your Inner Guardian will *become* you and you will become your Inner Guardian. You will begin to manifest and express the ideal *you* in more and more parts of your life.

And people will notice. They will comment on your changing. You will find others taking more interest in you. You will find yourself in a position to help others more often. You will more frequently find yourself feeling in control of your life. You will find yourself becoming increasingly creative and accomplishing more. You will find yourself succeeding more often than failing.

Imagine if...

- you had someone who could always guide you,

- you had someone who could help you
  make the right choices and correct decisions,

- the wisest person in the world were someone who
  truly knew about you and your situations, and

- you could call upon this person
  anytime and anywhere.

Such a person does exist.

IT IS YOU!

Listening to Your Inner Guardian (cont.)

This new you won't be without problems, but you will be able to handle them with greater ease. What problems you have won't get quite so complicated. You will have more confidence and be able to assert your will more easily. You will become more empowered.

When we learn to walk, we need someone to help us. At first it's a bit awkward. We stumble. We fall. We get frustrated. Eventually, though, walking becomes so natural we no longer even think about it.

Getting in touch with your Inner Guardian, your psychic and magical self, will seem strange and even awkward at first. You may feel like this isn't really working very well. But the more you practice and use your psychic abilities, the more you will be able to incorporate them into your everyday life. The more you work at them, the stronger the abilities become. Before long you are using your psychic powers whenever and wherever you wish without much thought about how to tap into them.

In this exercise, you will go quietly into meditation as described in "Creating Sacred Space" so you can meet and hear your Inner Guardian.

Magical Practice

Meeting Your Inner Guardian

- Set the mood.

- Perform a relaxation technique.

As you close your eyes, you see yourself standing in the Great Hall of a familiar castle. There is a feeling of peace and calm about. A part of you knows this inner castle is a sacred place—protected and full of wonders.

To your left is an arched door and you walk through it into an outer hallway. In this hallway is a beautiful spiral staircase and you head toward it.

As you begin to climb, you find yourself relaxing more and more. With each step, you leave the worries, stresses, and fears of your everyday life behind you. Soft candles light the stairway and as you go up the steps, a golden mist swirls a your feet.

When you reach the top of the stairs, you find yourself in a long hallway with only one door in the center. At the opposite end of the hallway another spiral staircase descends. The golden mist swirls and shimmers, hiding the floor of the hallway. As you walk through this golden mist, causing more swirls, a soft tinkling of bells seems to issue forth from it, sending shivers of delight through your body.

You reach down and stir the golden mist with your hands. You laugh at the wondrous colors and forms you create within it. You

Listening to Your Inner Guardian (cont.)

straighten up and move to the door. It is large and wooden, carved with many strange symbols and letters. You reach out with your hand and trace some of them. As you do, the door slowly opens inward, as if inviting you to enter.

Your eyes widen as you step across the threshold. You are standing in a large, circular room that looks like an ancient magician's laboratory. Around the walls are shelves of ancient books, manuscripts, and scrolls. There are collections of herbs, oils, and stones. Exotic plants grow in different parts of the room and seem to be watching you.

The ceiling is painted with a scene from the heavens and you gaze at the glistening stars. Then you realize the stars are moving, the sky shifting. You know the ceiling is enchanted, so if you wanted, you could trace the movements of the planets and stars in miniature.

Directly beneath the miniature sky is a globe of the earth. You watch it as it changes in response to the stars. As you stand looking at the globe, it becomes transparent and within it you see shadows of events around the world. A part of you realizes that here you could see how the stars might affect events and people upon the earth. You are amazed and make a note to yourself to come back and explore this further.

You smile and move further into the room. Feeling lighter and freer, you come to a full length mirror. As you stand before it, there is no reflection at all. This puzzles you, but then the faint outline of an ancient face appears in the mirror. This startles you and you take a step back. Then, softly, a voice speaks from that face in the mirror, "What is it you would see?"

You hesitate, unsure, and then say, "I wish to see my guardian."

"As you wish!" the voice replies and the mirror fills with misty clouds. The clouds shift and part, and you are amazed at the image that appears in the mirror. A magnificent person is standing there in the mirror, shining with great light! You tilt your head trying to see the image more clearly, and the person in the mirror tilts also. Only then do you realize the image in the mirror is the real you, the ideal you, the magical **you**—your Inner Guardian!

The eyes you see in the mirror—your eyes—are filled with wisdom. There is beauty, strength, and confidence radiating from you. As you gaze in wonder at the true essence of you, flashes of your abilities and potentials appear around the edges of the mirror. So many possibilities!

As you gaze upon your Inner Guardian, the light grows stronger and to your amazement, your Guardian steps out of the mirror and stands in front of you.

"I am the most creative part of you. I see that which you may ignore or not recognize. How may I help you?" The voice is soft and gentle, and there is nothing but complete acceptance of you and love for you. Your Inner Guardian motions for you to sit. As you do, your Guardian sits facing you. You think for a moment and then you begin to talk to your Guardian. You may ask about a problem. You may request some insight into a troubling area of your life. You may ask a question about the right action to take in a certain situation. You may ask about what is ahead for you in the coming week.

Your Guardian takes hold of both your hands and gazes deeply into your eyes. You both stand, your hands still held within your Guardian's. Then your hear your Guardian's answer. You listen and remember.

Listening to Your Inner Guardian (cont.)

"If you pay attention to the information I have offered and act accordingly, within a week you will see a change. Remember that I am you. I am always with you and each time we come together, I will become stronger and more of a blessing to you. I am the gift that is within you."

With your next breath, your Inner Guardian melts into you, coming to life stronger within you. You close your eyes, feeling your Inner Guardian—your true essence—awakening. You see and feel yourself stronger and more blessed. With each breath you take, your Inner Guardian grows in strength within you.

Your heart is filled with hope. There is no doubt that in the days ahead this magical part of you and all of its potentials will awaken more fully. You offer a prayer of thanks for this guidance.

You step away from the mirror and look about the room. So much to learn and explore! You smile, empowered, freer, and more magical. You step toward the door and it opens. You step into the golden mist of the hallway and now it swirls up around you like a golden cloak of magic. The mist has recognized what you have awakened.

As you make your way down the stairs, the hallway disappears behind you, and you inhale deeply, feeling very blessed. As you reach the bottom of the stairs, you find yourself back within your own room in your own sacred space. You are balanced, healed, blessed, and empowered.

Listening to Your Inner Guardian (cont.)

You look down at yourself and stretch, seeing yourself shining more brightly. Your magic and psychic powers are coming to life!

- **Perform a grounding ritual.**

In time all you will need to do is close your eyes and visualize your Inner Guardian.

Watch how your Guardian reacts to situations and people. Is it a positive reaction? Is it negative? Does your Guardian smile or frown?

By your Guardian's reaction you get clues as to what you should do and how you should respond to people and events around you.

You are
always
greater
than you
imagine!

SUGGESTIONS FOR PARENTS

➤ **Children do have spontaneous psychic experiences.**

These experiences are normal and can happen in a variety of ways. As parents, realize these experiences are often reminders of the potential within your young person. They can signal good times to start exploring and developing psychic capabilities.

Do treat such experiences as normal, though. Acknowledge the experiences and question the young person. Ask if the experience frightened your young person. If so, talk about it. Help them to see that it is a natural thing. Often bringing such experiences into the open is all that needs to be done to dissolve the fear.

Ask if your young person has had other experiences like this in the past. Discuss what happened. Try to help the young person understand. If you cannot, seek out legitimate and knowledgeable teachers and counselors in the psychic field to help in the understanding.

Use the experience as an opportunity to open some communication about exploring his or her psychic potentials further.

➤ **Allow the young person to proceed or not proceed further according to his or her comfort level.**

Exploration should never be forced.

➤ **Discuss your own hunches with the young person in your life.**

Explore if your hunches have been correct and what they might mean or how you might have misinterpreted them.

➤ **Create a sacred meditation time and place for you and your young person.**

Set aside a time for quiet—no television, no radio, no phone calls. Make this a quiet time for at least an hour. This time can be used for meditation, journalling, or some other creative activity.

Remember that any creative activity will help awaken intuitive abilities as long as it is enjoyable.

Lesson 2

The Art
of Divination

Wouldn't it be great to know the future?

Would it really help us?

Can we really know the future?

If we know the future, can we change it?

Dream interpretation. Reading tarot. Studying the stars. Watching for signs in nature. Consulting the Chinese I Ching. Dowsing with a pendulum. Gazing into a crystal ball.

Throughout the ages, people have tried to *divine,* or know, the future. Every society has had its practices, from the earliest of times to the present. Some of the past methods seem very strange to us today, but some of these very same methods are still being practiced.

Divination, often defined as fortune telling, is the receiving of knowledge as if it is coming from a divine source. Individuals who use divination are sometimes called seers, psychics, oracles, soothsayers, sensitives, and intuitives, just to name a few of the terms used. These are individuals who interpret events, answer questions about the future, make predictions, and uncover the truth. There are many types, forms, and expressions of divination. Everyone is different, and we all find some forms of psychic expression and some psychic tools easier for us to handle than others.

We are bombarded daily with so many sensory impressions that it's no wonder we ignore most of them. However, if you are in touch with your Inner Guardian, you have help in sorting out and recognizing which of all these impressions are important. For this reason, creating your own sacred space to connect with your Inner Guardian is very important.

Psych Out

**First Rule of Psychic Development:
Have fun!**

**Last Rule of Psychic Development:
Have fun!**

Your Inner Guardian talks to you through whatever form of psychic communication is easiest for you to receive. Some of you will dream about events. Some of you will see auras around people. Some of you will sense through touch. Some of you will receive visions from your Inner Guardians. Some of you may even be able to work with several or all of these ways of communicating with your Inner Guardian.

However, there are divination tools to further help your communication with your Inner Guardian. Some of the more common ones are tarot cards, astrology, and numerology, but there are many others. In this book we will learn about a variety of fun and simple methods for divining the future.

All these tools are easy to learn to use and with each use, your connection with your intuitive self will grow stronger. They will help you understand many of the things happening in your life, both the *what* and the *why*. These tools can help you solve problems, help you be more creative, and help you make more appropriate decisions and choices. Every time you use these tools, you increase your psychic power.

How Divination Works

Intuition and prophecy are all part of divination. They deal in some way with knowing the future, what is likely to unfold in someone's life. Some people roll their eyes and make fun of the possibility of seeing into the future. Others are afraid of this kind of psychic

You shape your
future by what
you do—
by the choices
you make and
the actions you take!

power. Those who are fearful often worry they will find out something bad is going to happen and are unaware that they often have the option of changing outcomes by exercising choice. Most people, however, are fascinated with the possibility of knowing their future.

You create possible futures by what you do or don't do in your life. If you study and prepare yourself for a particular kind of job, you are more likely to get that job than someone who doesn't. If you study for a test, you are more likely to pass it than someone who doesn't. You shaped your future by your choice of preparing for a particular job and by your decision to study.

If you skip studying for a test and go to a party instead, you have made a choice which may lead to your doing poorly on the test or even failing. You might get in trouble with your parents for going to a party instead of studying. On the other hand, you might meet someone at the party you never would have met if you had stayed home studying. Your different choices can lead to a variety of possibilities. We always create possibilities by our choices and actions and those possibilities shape our future.

A skilled psychic recognizes how our choices lead to opportunities. A good psychic knows that our actions in the past have set in motion certain possibilities for the present and future. With these in mind, psychics are able to read or divine what has brought us to where we are now and where things are likely headed for us if we continue making the same kinds of choices.

Psychic Absurdicus

Fun, Absurd, and Strange
Psychic Practices

ANTHROPOMANCY

This was the practice in Ancient Rome of consulting the intestines of sacrificed children in order to divine the future. The emperor Julian the Apostate was believed to have practiced this form of divination.

We change our future by changing our present behaviors and activities. Most people, however, remain unaware of how to change their behavior patterns even if they recognize them. Because of this, future possibilities are often easy to predict.

A friend of my wife used to call regularly every morning between 9:00 and 10:00 a.m. She was so regular about this it was easy to predict that when the phone rang during this time, it was probably her. She used to freak out when I'd answer the phone after the first ring with a "Hello, Donna." Because I knew her pattern of calling, it was easy to predict. To this day, she is still a little spooked by me. She never figured it out. (I enjoy the idea that I spook her a bit, so I've never told her.)

This wasn't really a psychic experience, but our Inner Guardian helps us to see these types of patterns so we can figure out possible outcomes. With divination, we receive help in seeing patterns so we can either reinforce those beneficial patterns or begin to change the troublesome ones as best we can.

Can We Know Our Future?

Yes, to a great degree. At the very least, we can learn to recognize future possibilities. We can begin to see what is likely to happen in our life if we continue living as we have been. We can also begin to see what is likely to happen if we make certain changes. The key to seeing these patterns and changing them is to establish a strong connection with our intuitive selves. We can begin by creating and using the sacred space we learned about in Lesson 1.

To understand how divination is possible, we must understand two basic principles at play our lives,

ALL THINGS ARE CONNECTED

Everything is connected to everything else. Every person is connected to every other person. Every event is linked to those of the past and to those of the future. Everything relates to everything else. This principle is known as the ancient Hermetic Law of Correspondence:

As above, so below;

As below, so above.

There is no such thing as coincidence.

Every action has a reaction. Everything we do and think sets energy into motion and shapes what will unfold somewhere within our life. Whatever we do will have some kind of result. The trick is figuring out how things relate. True divination comes from recognizing what those connections are or will be. Sometimes they will be

Calvin and Hobbes ©1993 Watterson. Reprinted with permission of Universal Press Syndicate. All rights reserved.

obvious. Other times it will take a great deal of effort to figure out these links and why things happen as they do. You will be able to increase your ability to identify these connections by creating and using your sacred space.

ALL THINGS ARE POSSIBLE…
BUT SOME ARE MORE PROBABLE

Not everything you psychically perceive or divine is set in stone. It is often a reflection of possibilities. Your impressions, dreams, images, visions, and psychic perceptions are usually *probable* patterns that are very likely to unfold. Your Inner Guardian guides your psychic power to help you see which events are more probable than others.

People who are strongly against fortune telling often give as a reason that it takes away our free will. People who confuse divination with fortune telling are really confusing fortune telling with fate and assuming fate is fixed and unchangeable. Fate, as we've talked about before, is not fixed. We always have free will.

As long as we are living in the physical world, there are going to be some events and situations we are not going to be able to change or to know about entirely. But if we can use our psychic abilities to divine probable outcomes, we can take actions or make changes that will make those outcomes more favorable to us.

Remember, we shape our future by what we choose to do. It is often said we can change our future by simply taking a different bus.

A Psychic Tale

Long ago, and not so long ago, there was a very sad frog. He was lonely and could not find a girl to take an interest in him. None of them ever seemed to want to know all about him as he did the girls.

He became so frustrated he did what any normal frog (or human, for that matter) would do. He called a psychic hotline. He told the psychic about his problem and frustration.

The psychic listened patiently. She said she would consult the spirits for the frog. He heard her mumbling and then say, "Yes, Yes. I see. I will tell the frog."

The frog was beginning to get very excited, and then he heard the psychic's voice speak softly.

"The spirits tell me that you will soon meet a young lady who will want to know everything about you."

The frog was thrilled. He began hopping up and down, beaming from ear-opening to ear-opening.

"Please, you've got to tell me. Who's it gonna be? When's it gonna be?" The frog could hardly contain his excitement.

There was a quiet pause on the phone line, and he listened to the psychic consulting with the spirits. Then her soft voice spoke to the frog.

"It will be next semester—in her biology class."

Tools of Divination

A very important part of developing psychic power is learning to use divination tools. These connect you with your Inner Guardian, much like a phone line, helping you to understand the messages more fully and with greater ease. These tools help you to develop and make the most of your psychic power. They are bridges to your Inner Guardian, providing you with wisdom, understanding, and insight.

Another way to look at divination tools is to think of them as a modem that links you to the Internet, expanding the possibilities for your computer. You are gaining greater access to information and knowledge. Divination tools help you to open up access to the "World Wide Web" of your psychic powers.

Divination tools can be particularly helpful when you are just beginning to awaken your psychic powers. One of the problems all psychics have is learning to trust in their perceptions and their interpretation of their psychic messages. It is always difficult to discern whether the psychic message is real or just something we want to hear. Divination tools help you to make these determinations. You become more objective and trusting of your psychic power when you have tools to help test your intuitions.

There are many types of divination tools to help awaken and connect to psychic power:

> *Astrology* studies the stars and planets to interpret how their movements affect our life.

> *Tarot cards* come in a variety of forms and use their unique symbols to help us interpret and understand events in our lives.

> *Numerology* is based on the idea that everything is governed by mathematics. By interpreting the numbers in names and birth dates, life path and potentials can be revealed.

> *Dreams* use images and scenarios to communicate messages.

> *Pendulums* bridge the outer life of electrical impulses to the inner self. Interpreting the pendulum movements gives answers to questions.

Throughout this book you will have a chance to explore and practice some common tools of divination as well as some uncommon but very effective ones. All divination tools have their benefits, but as you explore and practice them for awakening your psychic power, you will find some work easier for you than others.

Most people know of me through my work with animals, totems, and reading the signs of nature. When I want to get an idea about how projects are unfolding and how the rhythms in my life are playing out, I take an answer-walk through nature looking for signs. If I am having difficulty being objective (and we all do sometimes), I will use the tarot or the Chinese I Ching, an ancient form of divination. It can be quite complicated, but I have found it provides great insight into problems. For me, it is especially good at getting insight into behind-the-scenes activities I may not be aware of in my life.

A lot of times I use a form of divination known as *bibliomancy*. I will take a moment to quiet myself, thinking about a particular problem or question. Then I randomly take a book off my shelf and open it to any page. Most of the time the page I turn to has an answer or some form of guidance that I can use.

In time, you will not need these tools. You will have established such a strong connection to your psychic powers that you can draw on them at any time, anywhere. Until then, it is a good idea to explore and learn to use several tools, finding out which ones work best for you in understanding and interpreting the psychic messages from your Inner Guardian.

Knowing yourself
and all of
your magical
possibilities
is the most
important step in
seeing and
shaping your future.

Understanding the Message

Receiving the psychic message is the easy part. Understanding it is what's hard. The subconscious mind controls over 90 percent of our body's activities. It also monitors and registers everything that goes on around us. Your Inner Guardian takes all of the information stored in the subconscious and tries to pass any of it on to you that is important for you to know.

This seems simple enough, doesn't it? Well, not really. There's a small problem. Your Inner Guardian has no language ability. It can't speak like you do when you want to tell your friends something. Your Inner Guardian has to find other ways of communicating with you and this is where divination tools come in handy.

Your Inner Guardian usually communicates to you through symbols and images. It can send you pictures through dreams, through tarot cards, through your imaginings—whatever way it can reach you the best with whatever images and symbols you might understand. Your task is to figure out what those images and symbols mean.

All symbols and images will be **personal**, having a meaning unique to you. An acorn may be "the seed from which grows the mighty oak" to many people, but maybe as a child someone threw an acorn at you and hit you in the head. To you, the acorn represents pain and possibly an attack by someone. Your Inner Guardian knows this and will use your personal associations with this image to communicate with you.

Guide to Interpreting Symbols

➤ **Always begin with what the image means to you.**

Your Inner Guardian will try to use images and symbols
it knows you can relate to. Ask yourself some simple
questions about the image. What do you think about
when you think of this thing? What does it bring to
mind? How does that fit with what is going on around
you? What emotion does it stir in you?

➤ **Trust your first impression.**

It will almost always be partly accurate. Then consult
other possibilities. How would other sources (books and
people) interpret these symbols or images? What do
they mean to others? Do these symbols have a common
meaning to people in general?

➤ **Focus on what the message is and not when it will
happen.**

Determining the timing of possible events is one of the
most difficult part of psychic development. When we
are first developing our psychic abilities, when things
happen is not as important as what is likely to happen.
Determining what the message is should be your focus.
In time and with *lots* of practice, you will begin to get a
feel for how to figure out the timing.

➤ **Create a dictionary of interpretations.**

In your Book of Enchantment (see Volume I of this
series), keep track of the images and what they mean to
you. In time, their meanings will deepen and grow. In
this way you develop your own dictionary of symbols.

In the beginning, it is easy to misinterpret these pictorial messages. Sometimes the images will be very literal. You dream of getting caught cheating at school and low and behold, you do get caught. On the other hand, maybe you draw the tarot card called Death. Some people are really fearful of this card, believing it literally means someone is going to die. This tarot card does NOT mean death literally. It refers instead to a transition, the ending of one thing and the beginning of another. This card means there is change coming into your life.

Interpreting your psychic communications accurately takes lots of practice. You must keep track of what you think things mean and how you feel about them at the time. If your feelings prove to be accurate, then the next time you have a similar communication, you will more easily be able to interpret its meaning. You will have gained clarity in seeing the message. The table on page 70 provides some useful guidelines for beginning to work with symbols and figuring out their meanings as they apply to your life.

When I first started college, I thought I would make myself look older if I started smoking. I smoked for about ten years before I smartened up and quit. Periodically, I dream about smoking again. It always signals that I am becoming obsessed with something I am working on or that I am starting to develop a bad habit about something. This dream is a part of my own personal dictionary of symbols.

center
Magical Practice

Cloud Readings

skills developed
- increases understanding of symbols
- helps develop clairvoyance

Remember lying back in the grass and looking up at the clouds? How many different things can you see in clouds? Like a Rorschach ink-blot test, clouds will take on many formations. Your Inner Guardian will help you to see images which answer your questions.

Cloud reading is one of the oldest forms of divination and was commonly practiced among the Celtics and the Druids. By looking at the formations and how the clouds moved, fortunes could be determined.

When I attended an International New Age Trade Show, one of my books, *Animal-Wise*, had been submitted for the organization's awards contest. On the bus from the hotel to the awards banquet, I was doing some cloud watching, quietly wondering whether my book would win an award that night. As I gazed out the window, I saw four very large dragons in the cloud formations. In the Eastern part of the world, dragons are good luck, reflecting good fortune and great power. I felt then

left

RORSCHACH INK BLOTS

What do these remind you of?

*Ink blots are made by dabbing ink onto paper and then folding
the paper in half. The mind tries to make sense of these
images, and so what you "see" can be quite revealing.
To practice developing your psychic abilities, think about
a question and then stare at the ink blots.
Trust your imagination and your Inner Guardian
to help you see what applies to your question.*

that I would win an award that night. However, I sure hadn't connected the number four with the four awards *Animal-Wise* won that night, including Book of the Year!

Cloud readings are a wonderful way to practice understanding your Inner Guardian and its symbols. When I participated in psychic fairs, many of those put on in the spring and summer were held outdoors. At times I would do cloud readings for people just to do something different. I would take the person's hand in mine and then look to the clouds. My Inner Guardian would then help me to see images that related to the person I was reading for.

When you are ready to practice cloud reading, pick a time when there are plenty of clouds. It's particularly fun if you can lay back in the grass. You can also do it spontaneously, such as I did on the bus to the awards banquet.

Remember, you will see and feel what your Inner Guardian knows you can relate to. With every cloud divination, you strengthen your ability to work with your Inner Guardian and develop your psychic power. By learning how to use this technique, you've got a tool you can use anywhere as long as there are clouds in the sky.

Cloud Readings (cont.)

1. **Relax.**

    Quiet and center yourself. For this particular activity you do not need to create a formal sacred space. Take a few moments, though, to think of all of Nature as a sacred place.

    If you wish to create a formal space, do so in the manner described earlier.

2. **Close your eyes and think of a question or a problem.**

    Sometimes it helps to ask the "cloud spirits" for assistance.

3. **As you look to the clouds, pay attention to any formation.**

    Your Inner Guardian will help you to recognize images that relate to your particular questions.

4. **When a cloud formation catches your eye, ask yourself some questions:**

    What does that image mean to me?

    Is it positive or negative?

    What could this image mean to people in general?

5. **Trust in any emotions you feel.**

Magical Practice

Color My World

| **skills developed** | • promotes understanding the meaning of colors
• helps in divining the moods of others |

Colors express energy, so can enter into many forms of magic and healing. Color is a dynamic part of our life and our culture, speaking to us and affecting us in many different ways. Because of this, color is a tool your Inner Guardian will frequently use to communicate.

Each color has its own unique qualities. Some are exciting and some soothing. Some stimulate mental activity and some aid in healing. Some are depressing and some protective. We all have colors we like and dislike.

Many believe we subconsciously pick colors we know will help us throughout our day. Your Inner Guardian guides you to those colors. Ever wonder why the clothes you pick out for the next day don't quite seem right in the morning? You have had time to rest and those colors are no longer your most beneficial on this new day.

In this magical practice, you are learning to divine the moods of others by the colors they wear. It will help you to learn the meaning of colors, giving you another tool for interpreting psychic communications from your Inner Guardian.

Reading Colors

1. **Begin to get in the habit of looking at colors as a reflection of a person's mood or character.**

   Look at others on the school bus or in your classroom. What color are they wearing? Do they wear that color frequently?

2. **Does the color worn reveal the person's character or is it a balancing color?**

   Trust your impressions on this.

   Sometimes people choose an opposite color to balance something about themselves. For example, people who are usually very mental and heavy thinkers (a yellow quality) will occasionally be drawn to blues. The blue helps calm all of that excessive thinking.

In time you will begin to recognize basic qualities and moods of people by the colors they wear. The table on the following pages provides some attributes of color. You will begin to divine some insight into people no matter how they present themselves.

What Colors

RED

color of power and strength; linked to sexual energy; can indicate an active person with lots of energy; darker shades can reflect strong emotions and even anger; can also indicate a creative person.

ORANGE

often indicates love of fun; creativity; person often shows generosity but may be overly so and tire easily; bright and optimistic.

YELLOW

friendly and alert with a great deal of mental activity; may not know how to relax; eager learners and curious; prefer to lead and can be a bit willful.

GREEN

color of healing and balance; peaceful; if drawn to greens, person probably looking for some emotional balance; naturally compassionate and friendly; honest and helpful.

BLUE

color of spiritual understanding; usually very perceptive; if drawn to blue, person may be looking for calm; often deeply involved in their work, sometimes neglecting other things; dedicated and talented, but can also be fault-finding.

Color My World (cont.)

Do You Wear?

PURPLE AND VIOLET	seekers; can be impatient with others, including themselves; usually successful and have high ideals, but person can become depressed if ideals not met; need and seek spiritual experiences in life and this where they find their power.
BLACK	not a negative color, but of protection and groundedness; worn by sensitive individuals; person can be quite psychic; when worn with another color, strengthens the other color; can also indicate secretiveness; a color of quiet strength.
WHITE	color of spirit and of balance; wearing mostly white with little or no other color may indicate a person with difficulty relating to others; hopeful; can have strong religious or spiritual beliefs; when worn with other colors, amplifies the other color's qualities.
BROWN	color of a person who is down-to earth, practical minded and very helpful; indicates ability to develop quick and strong friendships; often devoted workers, but can be overly critical; strong and noble.

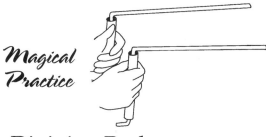

Magical
Practice

Divining Rods

skills
developed

- increases intuition
- promotes better awareness of your psychic powers

In Volume I of this series, *Magic of Believing,* we learned how to use a pendulum to get answers to questions and even to locate lost things. Pendulums are tools of a science known as *radiethesia* or *dowsing.* Divining rods (also called dowsing rods) are another tool of this kind of divination.

Divining rods have been used in war time to locate mines. Some modern utility companies teach their workers to use them to find the buried lines needing repairs. They have been used all over the world to find underground water and mineral deposits. People who use divining rods for these purposes used to be called "water witches."

Divining rods, like the pendulum, are wonderful tools for tapping into the psychic parts of us. Just like the pendulum, they reach the magical part of our mind. When we ask the psychic part of ourselves a question, an electrical signal is sent in answer, traveling through the nervous system to deliver a message—much like over a phone line. This causes an involuntary muscle movement (one that we cannot control). This in turn causes the divining rods to open or close, giving us answers to our questions.

MAKING DIVINING RODS

Making divining rods is simple. Old timers used a willow branch shaped like a Y, holding the two legs of Y in their hands and pointing the stem of the Y away from them. They then watched and felt which way the stem moved. If they were seeking underground water sources, the stem would dip down toward the ground when water was there.

Instead of a Y-shaped rod, we will learn how to make and use L-shaped rods.

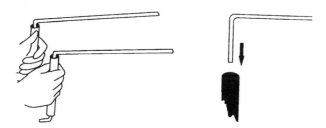

1.   Take a simple metal clothes hanger and cut it or bend it so it forms the shape of an L.

     The long end of the L should be 8 to 12 inches. The short end should be 3 to 6 inches. You can also use a thin piece of copper wire or some other moldable metal rod.

2. **Take a piece of thin cardboard and roll it up into a tight circle that can slide over the small end of the L.**

   Make the cardboard as tight a roll as possible without it fitting too snugly on the small end of the L. It should be loose enough that the hanger or wire can spin freely, but tight enough to hold the rods securely.

   Once you've gotten the cardboard rolled they way you want it, tape it in this rolled up position. Many dry cleaner hangers have a cardboard roll on the bottom portion. These can be cut to make a handle that is firm, but allows the metal hanger itself to move freely.

3. **Slide the cardboard handle over the small end of the L so that at least one inch of the hanger sticks out.**

   Bend this one-inch extension about 90 degrees so the handle stays in place.

4. **Repeat steps 1 through 3 to make a second divining rod so you have one for each hand.**

5. **Get a feel for the rods by swirling them around. They should move freely within the handle.**

   Hold the rods lightly in your hands. Bend your arms at the elbow so that your hands and the rods are about chest level.

   The rods should be able to swing in a complete circle without touching any part of your body. The tips should be slightly pointed down and about six to eight inches apart.

Divining Rods (cont.)

Programming the Divining Rods

After you have made your set of divining rods, you will need to decide what you want the swinging in and out of the rods to mean. I use the opening of the rods to mean a *yes,* or a positive response, and a closing of the rods to mean a *no*, or negative response. Decide on this ahead of time. Always be consistent with these designations whenever you use your divining rods.

1. **Hold the rods in front of you and think of the word** *yes***.**

    Say out loud, "When I ask a question and the answer is *yes*, the rods will swing outward." If you have to, coax them outward. You are training the rods to work with your psychic powers.

2. **Let the rods come back to their starting position and think of the word** *no***.**

    Say out loud, "When I ask a question and the answer is *no*, the rods will swing inward." If you have to, coax them into the inward position. Practice this for about ten minutes a day for a week or two or until they start moving in the direction you wish them to. It won't take you long to get the hang of them.

Testing Your Divining Rods

When your divining rods move the way you want them to to indicate yes and no, you are ready to test them.

1. **Ask yourself some *yes* and *no* questions.**

   Keep them simple.

   > Is my name _____?

   > Do I have a brother/sister?

   > Do I like _____?

   > Does _____ like me?

   > Will I have a surprise quiz in math tomorrow?

   > Will I rule the world?

   > *(O.K., this last one may be too much to ask of the rods, sending them into wild and crazy movements or possibly frying them.)*

2. **Continue testing your divining rods each day for 10 to 15 minutes for a week.**

   Ask questions for yourself and others.

   Experiment. HAVE FUN!

Divining Rods (cont.)

Testing Your Divining Rods (cont.)

3. **Try forecasting the weather.**

   Your subconscious is very much aware of changes in the atmosphere around you. It can help you to recognize good and bad weather coming your way.

   Take a map of the United States and as you guide the rods over each area, ask the rods to point out where bad weather will occur. (I like to use crossed rods for bad weather and open rods for good weather.)

4. **Try measuring how good or bad foods are for you.**

   A number of people use divining rods to help them decide on vitamins and foods their body needs. They hold the rods over the particular foods or vitamins and ask if they are needed at this time.

   Your Inner Guardian knows what your body needs and can communicate this to you through the movement of the rods. (I've found that my body pretty much always needs potato chips—whether the rods say so or not.)

MEASURING AURAS

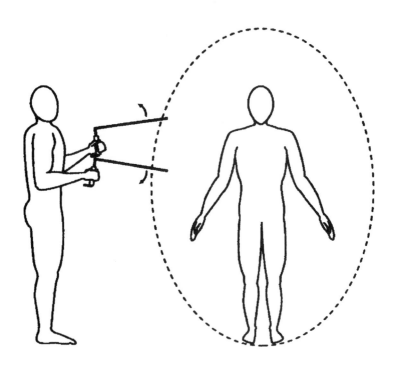

Divining Rods (cont.)

MEASURING AURAS (cont.)

Measure the aura of friends and family. Measure the auras of your pets. Pay attention to how the energies change in different situations.

1. Stand about 15 to 20 feet back from another person.

2. Holding the divining rods in front of you, as if you are aiming at the person.

3. Slowly walk toward the person while holding the rods out in front of you.

    The dowsing rods will open wider, swinging out as they come in contact with the outer edge of the person's aura.

    The person's aura extends that far around the person in all directions.

Practice measuring auras at different times of the day and with different people when they are in different moods. This helps you to learn to use the rods with more skill and helps you to see how our energy fields change throughout the day.

SUGGESTIONS FOR PARENTS

➤ **Explore the symbols in your own life with your young person.**

What do the clothes you wear say about you? Or your hair style? What about the car you drive? The house you live in?

➤ **Do ink-blot readings with each other.**

Make your own ink blots with your young person. You could even try making them from different colors.

➤ **Take a divination class together.**

Many stores offer workshops on astrology, palm reading, tarot, and other divination techniques.

➤ **Take a people-watching trip to your local mall or airport.**

Try and determine the mood of people by what color they are wearing. Try and determine their personality or job by how they are dressed.

Discuss how people's appearance affects how others treat them.

➤ **Together, make a set of divining rods.**

Take a trip to the local hardware store and purchase the supplies to make a fancier pair than those from hangers. You will be surprised at what you can come up with by walking the aisles of the hardware store.

Lesson 3

Magic Touch

Have you ever shaken hands and known immediately whether you like the person or not?

Have you ever walked into a room and known immediately something had been going on?

Have you ever felt relaxed and calmed by a friend's touch?

Do some places make you feel comfortable and others make you feel ill at ease?

Have you ever felt someone's presence without actually seeing the person?

Do you get caught up in the moods of those around you?

Do you know when your belongings are out of place or have been picked up by someone?

We've all used psychic touch throughout our lives, but many people just don't realize it. Psychic touch is the ability to get intuitive insight and information through our sense of touch by "feeling" what's around us.

Our ability to sense things through our feelings is actually quite amazing. Our skin is our largest sensory organ. Surrounding our skin is our *aura*, the mostly invisible blend of various kinds of energies about all living things. Our skin and our aura work together to register everything we come in contact with, no matter how subtle, including things in our environment. Most of what our skin and aura picks up gets shuffled into the subconscious mind, but we can easily learn to pay attention to what we "feel" around us.

About Auras

The human body is absolutely magnificent! It gives off heat, light, sound, electricity, and even magnetic frequencies. It is in every sense of the words an energy system and these energies surrounding the human body form the human aura.

All living things have auras. In the average person, the aura extends in all directions for eight to ten feet. The divining rods we made in Lesson 2 can be used to measure a person's aura. It is the qualities of this energy field, our aura, which are largely responsible for making psychic touch possible.

Imprinting Through Our Aura

The aura is predominantly electro-magnetic energy. We are constantly giving off energy in an electrical form and absorbing energy in a magnetic form through our auras. This energy exchange occurs between people, plants, animals, objects and places—with just about anything. Through our aura, we leave imprints of ourselves where we visit and on things we touch, especially on our personal spaces and personal items.

We exchange energy with everyone we encounter throughout the day. If we are around a lot of people, we will have exchanged a lot of energy, which can make us tired. This energy exchange can also cause us to have a lot of strange thoughts and ideas running around in our heads. There's nothing wrong with us—we're not going crazy. Our auras have just picked up some of the "energy debris" of those around us.

This picking up and giving off of energy is called *imprinting*. We leave traces of our energy everywhere: on our books, on our jewelry, on our desks at school, and even in our rooms. It is like a kind of energy static cling. Through psychic touch, we can learn to "read" this imprint.

STRENGTHENING THE IMPRINT

The longer and more direct our contact with something, the greater the energy imprint we leave upon it. Photographs and personal items become links to us, quite literally, because of these imprints we leave behind.

If your family has ever moved, you know how long it takes before the new place starts to feel like home. It takes time to put your imprint on this new space. A good psychic can tune into a person's imprint on personal objects or living space. As a person no longer

Psychic Science

HOLOGRAMS

Holograms are three-dimensional images. You may have seen movies or television shows in which lifelike images are projected to trick people. You may also have seen hologram images on cards, bookmarks, and even credit cards. When you move these images, they become more lifelike, appearing to be more three-dimensional.

At Stanford University, scientists experimented with holograms to document their characteristics. They took holographic photos of things such as a horse. Then they cut out a piece of the photo, such as part of the nose, and enlarged it to the size of the original.

What do you think happened?

Did they get just a large version of the horse's nose?

No! What happened was amazing! When the scientists enlarged the small piece of the horse's photograph, they got a picture of the whole horse—not just a large nose! And the same thing happened with every piece of every holographic photo they enlarged.

So what did this demonstrate to the scientists?

This showed scientists how the part is connected to the whole and the whole is contained in the part. It also helps explain how, in the world of psychic phenomena, a part of something such as a person's leaving a mere trace of energy on an object in the form of an energy imprint can give information about the whole person.

THIS MAKES
PSYCHIC TOUCH POSSIBLE!

maintains contact with objects or places, the imprints quickly fade away, usually replaced by the imprints of those now associated with them.

No Two Auras are Alike

Your aura is like an energy fingerprint. No two auras are ever exactly alike because we each have our own unique energy frequencies. This makes our imprints recognizable as belonging to a particular person. Your bedroom feels different from your brother's, sister's, or your parent's rooms because of your own unique energy patterns. This is why you can tell your ring from one that looks similar to it. This is how you know your little brother or sister has been messing with your stuff.

How Psychic Touch Works

When we have psychic touch experiences, we take in information in a variety of ways. In this lesson, we will focus on holding someone's object and while relaxing, trying to read the imprints on it. This can be done to learn about the person. The object helps you to connect with the owner's spirit guides. You can even read what kind of day this person has had. There are no limits.

When we tune into an object or a place, we ask our Inner Guardian to read the imprints and pass that information on to us. Now remember, your Inner Guardian cannot speak or use language. It must find some way to help you understand and one way it does this is to stimulate physical feelings. Your Inner Guardian may also stir up within you the same emotions imprinted on the object or place. Your Inner Guardian may create images in your mind relating to the object's imprint.

PHYICAL SENSATIONS

With psychic touch, you will always have some kind of **physical** sensation. You may feel warm or cold. You may feel a change in pressure, as if the air is getting thicker. You may notice a part of your body itch. Or tingle. Or ache. By relaxing and paying attention to what you feel physically, you start to connect with the imprints on the object.

When you first pick up an object, pay attention to what you feel and where on your body you feel it. Ask yourself the following kinds of questions:

➤ Do you feel tightness in the neck?
  Maybe the person is having a lot of stress.

➤ Do you feel warm and fuzzy or cold and distant?

➤ Is there an itching around the knee?
  Maybe the person is recovering from an injury.

In the beginning, just pay attention to what you feel and where. In the magical practices in this lesson, you will learn how to start translating and interpreting the feelings you get from imprints.

EMOTIONAL SENSATIONS

Sometimes the imprint will create an **emotional response** within us. Humans are very emotional beings,

The Necklace

The psychic holds the girl's necklace in her hands, closing her eyes and breathing deeply. As the psychic relaxes, she begins to pay attention to what she feels. She lets her Inner Guardian read the imprints on the jewelry and give her information about the owner and about the necklace's history.

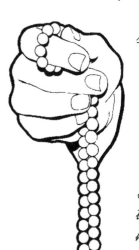

The psychic has a warm, tingling sensation. Then she sees a flash of color and an image of an older woman, someone in her eighties. She feels strong, loving protective emotions all around what she sees in that flash.

The psychic then begins to translate what she has experienced into words the young girl can understand. The necklace was a gift of love, passed down from mother to daughter in the family for several generations. It came from an older woman—the girl's great-grandmother. The psychic describes the woman and the great love she had for her family and how that love continues from the spirit world even to this day. . . .

and we actually feel the emotions of others. Ask yourself the following kinds of questions about your feelings:

➤ Do you start to feel happy or tense? Depressed? Silly?

➤ Do you feel a little goofy?
(Don't worry; we all do at times when we start doing these kinds of things.)

Your Inner Guardian will try and help you feel the emotion imprinted on this object, usually the one most recently and most often experienced by the owner.

VISUAL IMAGES

Sometimes your Inner Guardian will help you to see things associated with the object. You will get **visual messages**. You may see colors. You may see people or images of various kinds. You may even just have some thoughts pass through your mind relating to the object:

➤ What color comes to mind as you hold this object?
Trust in what you imagine even if you can't actually "see" the color.

➤ Are there people associated with the object? Are they male or female?

➤ Are there other images, thoughts, or scenarios that come to mind as you hold this object within your hands?

The difficulty is in interpreting the images. Remember, your Inner Guardian will always use images and thoughts it knows you can relate to and understand. If you ask the questions, the Inner Guardian will give you the answers!

*Magical
Practice*

It's All in the Hands

**skills
developed**
- awakens psychic touch
- increases sensitivity of the hands

Healers and psychics often use this exercise in their work. It stimulates the sensory centers of the hands, enabling them to more easily use their hands to sense and feel subtle energies in people and in objects.

This exercise awakens the sensitivities of your hands and should be used before any activities involving psychic touch. With this exercise, you will begin to feel and sense the energies of people and objects with much greater ease.

Do not worry that you might be imagining what you are sensing. You are working to begin to recognize these subtle energies.

SENSITIZING YOUR HANDS

- Perform a progressive relaxation.

- Create your sacred space.

1. **Rub the palms of your hands together briskly for about 30 seconds.**

   This stimulates their overall sensitivity.

2. **Extend your hands about a foot and a half in front of you.**

   Your palms should be facing each other about two feet apart.

3. **Slowly move your hands toward each other, bringing them as close to each other as you can without touching them.**

4. **Then slowly draw your hands back so they are about six to eight inches apart.**

It's All in the Hands (cont.)

5. **Repeat this in and out movement of your hands for several minutes.**

   As you do, pay attention to what you feel or sense. There are a variety of possibilities:

   ✓ feeling pressure building between the hands,

   ✓ a tickling sensation,

   ✓ a feeling of thickness between the palms,

   ✓ a sense of changing temperature, a warming or cooling between your hands, or even

   ✓ a pulsing or soft throbbing sensation.

   If you were practicing on an object, at this point you would then take the object into your hand.

• **Perform a grounding ritual.**

Take time to record your responses in your Book of Enchantment.

If you can
imagine it,
you can
know it and
you can be it.

Magical Practice

Feeling the Aura

skills developed

- improves psychic touch
- helps to feel our energy beyond skin level
- sensitizes us to the human aura

After learning to energize your hands and stimulate their sensitivity in the previous magical practice, you are now ready to take your psychic touch a step further.

This exercise can be performed by yourself as you learn to sense your own aura. However, you might find practicing with a partner works better for you. Directions are given for sensing your own aura or for working with a partner to sense each other's aura.

Sensing Your
Own Aura

- Create your sacred space.

- Perform a progressive relaxation.

1. **Energize your hands by rubbing them together for 60 seconds.**

   You are using the same procedure as in the previous magical practice, "It's All in the Hands."

2. **Hold your dominant hand about 12 inches above your bared opposite forearm and begin moving your hand back and forth over your forearm.**

   As in the previous exercise, you will begin to sense the energy surrounding your forearm without actually touching it (which you want to avoid).

   This may be a feeling of thickness, a feeling of a change in temperature, of a feeling of pressure building.

3. **Try moving your hand back and forth over other parts of the body.**

   This is just to get you used to sensing your energy field. Try switching hands. Practice with each hand about 5 to 10 minutes per session.

- **Perform a grounding ritual.**

Magical Practice

SENSING THE AURA OF
ANOTHER PERSON

- Decide who will be going first with sensing the other's aura.

- Together, create a sacred space.

1. The person who's aura will be sensed sits in a chair.

    The person sensing the aura stands behind and raises both hands about
    12 to 18 inches above the head of the seated person.

2. The person doing the sensing first stands behind the chair and rubs his or her hands together to sensitize them.

3. As in the previous exercise, the person standing behind the chair begins by slowly moving his or her hands up and down, close to the head and shoulders of the person sitting in the chair.

    Be careful not to touch the person as you run your hands up and down, one on each side of the person.

    Every one's head has strong energy emanating from it, so the head is one of the easiest parts of the body for feeling and sensing the aura.

Feeling the Aura (cont.)

4. **Move your hands up and down your partner's head and shoulders for about three minutes.**

   You will begin to feel changes. These may be the same thickening or pulsing energy you've felt before. Or warmth or coolness. Pay attention to anything you feel or sense.

   Do not worry that you may be imagining what you are feeling. Make a mental note of all that you feel and experience

5. **Discuss with your partner what you experienced.**

   The more feedback you get, the better.

6. **Switch places with your partner and repeat the steps.**

• **Perform a grounding ritual.**

Part of the grounding can be comparing experiences. Record these experiences in your Books of Enchantment.

Magical Practice

Reading Objects

skills
developed

- increases psychic ability through the sense of touch
- develops ability to communicate psychic messages more clearly

Working with a small group of friends is a wonderful way to develop psychic touch. Regular psychic touch get-togethers provide lots of opportunities to practice and there is more feedback than usual. Such get-togethers can be great fun!

Group members can bring different objects from home. Then other members of the group can practice psychic touch on those objects. Make sure that the objects are something that you know about. The feedback is what develops your skills.

Each member of the group brings a small object, something that can fit in the hands, and places it in a small, plain white envelope so no one sees what the others brought. This way there is no clue what the object is and you have to rely on your own psychic abilities.

Group Readings

- **As a group, create your sacred space.**

With a group, the person whose home is used can be the leader or each member of the group can take a turn. He or she will then be responsible for helping to set the mood, bringing candles, appropriate music, etc.

- **As a group, perform a relaxation technique.**

The leader for each session can lead the others in a relaxation.

1. **All members take one of the envelopes.**

    Open the envelope to make sure you did not get your own object. If you did, trade with someone else.

2. **All members energize their hand sensitivity by rubbing their palms together for 60 seconds.**

3. **All members take the objects in their envelopes out and put them between their hands, close their eyes, and relax.**

4. **Everyone attunes to the object in their hands by paying attention to physical, emotional, and visual sensations as they hold the object.**

Magical Practice

5. **Begin by concentrating on physical feelings, making a mental note of any you may be having.**

   Do you feel hot or cold? Does a part of your body itch? What part of the body comes to mind, even if you don't feel anything there?

   Trust what you are feeling.

6. **Next, concentrate on what emotions you are feeling.**

   What kind of day has the owner of this object had? Stressful? Happy? Silly? What kind of emotion feels strongest about this object's owner?

   If you do not feel any emotion or feel the emotion is bizarre, trust what you imagine. If you have to pick an emotion that reflects this person, what emotion first comes to mind?

7. **Next, concentrate on what images come to mind.**

   Begin with colors. Are there any colors that come to mind? If there is a color, what would you imagine it to be, even if you don't actually see the color? You could not imagine the color if it did not have some reality to it. What does that color mean to you?

   Are there any people? Spirit guides?

Reading Objects (cont.)

8. **When you are finished sensing anything and every-thing you can about the object, write down all of your impressions—everything you felt—on the envelope.**

   As you begin writing down your impressions, it is common to come up with even more information and ideas. Write theses things down too. They often help you to clarify some of the impressions.

9. **Share your psychic touch experience with the owner of the object.**

   Get as much detail and feedback as possible. To-gether, try to figure out the things you felt but did not understand.

   By getting feedback, the next time something similar happens, you will have a better idea of how to inter-pret the feeling or image.

10. **Keep a record of the results of your psychic touch practice.**

    You will be surprised how accurate you become and how quickly!

- **Perform a grounding ritual.**

Part of the grounding can be sharing your experi-ences with each other. If someone seemed less suc

Magical Practice

Reading Objects (cont.)

cessful than the others, the rest of the group can sometimes encourage more response with some questioning:

Did you feel anything, even if you only imagined it? The more someone talks, even if only about "feeling nothing," the more the information actually comes out. Talking about it actually brings out the information.

The leader can further help the group ground by guiding them through some stretching movements and even providing some light snacks. The leader should also remind everyone this is not a contest. The goal is to have fun!

The group can do several of these exercises. Keep them simple and short, about 15 to 20 minutes each. If you decide to do a second or third object, wash your hands between sessions. Otherwise, when you use psychic touch on the new objects, your hands will still have the residue from the previous object on them, which can confuse what you experience.

GUIDLINES FOR
READING IMPRINTS

➤ Close your eyes when you take the object between your hands.

➤ Attune to the object, noting and describing any physical sensations, emotions, or images.

➤ Attend to what colors you imagine as you hold the object.

➤ Talk with the owner of the object about what you are sensing, no matter how bizarre it may seem. Let the owner help you understand what you felt and why.

➤ Record your results in your Book of Enchantment or a notebook just for your readings so you can track your progress.

Magical Practice

Psychic Touch Games

skills developed
- develops psychic touch
- increases touch sensitivities

The best way to develop any psychic ability is to practice, but there's no reason you can't have fun doing it! To develop psychic touch, there are wonderful games that can be played alone or with others.

In the first, you will be working with a deck of cards to sense whether you can tell the black cards from the red cards.

In the second game you will be working with old photographs to try to sense information about the people in them.

Sensing the Color of Cards

With ordinary playing cards, practice trying to sense the colors of the suits. Every color has an energy, a feel to it. Through psychic touch, we will try and feel whether the card is red or black.

- Create your sacred space.

1. Energize your hands by rubbing your palms together for 60 seconds.

2 Take one red card and turn it face up so you can see the color.

3. Place your hands about 3 to 6 inches above the card, close your eyes, and pay attention to anything you feel.

4. Repeat steps 2 and 3 with one black card.

5. Shuffle the deck of cards and set it face down in front of you.

6. Put one of the cards in the deck face down on the table in front of you and try to feel whether the card is red or black.

7. Turn the card over and see if you were correct.

8. Repeat with another card.

   You will be surprised how quickly you improve with practice.

Magical Practice

SENSING PEOPLE IN PHOTOGRAPHS

We usually have an emotional response to friends and so identifying people we know in photographs through psychic touch often involves paying attention to the emotion or feeling we get.

Gather a stack of photographs of people in your life. Start with people you know because they will give you a stronger response than something like vacation scenery shots. Try to keep the photos all about the same size so shape doesn't give any clues.

WHO ARE THEY

- Create your sacred space

1. Energize your hands by rubbing your palms together for about 60 seconds.

2. Mix up the of photos and take one from the stack, keeping the image face down.

Psychic Touch Games (cont.)

3. **Either hold the photograph between your hands or place your hands about three to six inches above the photo as it lays on a flat surface in front of you.**

4. **Close your eyes and pay attention to what you feel.**

   Is there a a particular emotion that wells up? Do you feel anything physical? Who do you feel is in the photograph?

   Take about one to two minutes with each photograph if necessary, but no longer.

5. **Turn the photo over to check yourself.**

   Remembering how you felt while sensing this picture will help you identify and pinpoint photos more accurately the next time.

• **Perform a grounding ritual.**

Magical Practice

The Empathic Reading

skills developed
- heightens ability to feel psychically
- develops the ability to tune in quickly
- increases control of psychic feeling

We have all imagined what it would be like to be someone else. This is a form of *empathy*, a heightened kind of feeling. We feel what other living things feel, both the joys and the pains. If you have ever taken on the attitudes and behaviors of others without realizing it, talking like them or acting like them, you have experienced empathy.

Empathy can be developed so strongly that just by touching someone, you can feel and experience what that person feels and experiences. With empathy this strong, we can really get to know about the person, but it takes a lot of control to be able to do this.

Some people are more naturally empathic than others and need to be careful about becoming too sensitive. In Lesson 7 we will explore more about how to recognize and control it.

Imagine if...

- you could touch someone and know everything about the person,

- you could take someone's aches and pains away just by touching them, or

- you were able to know what is behind the masks others wear.

Magical Practice

This exercise helps you to develop control over your psychic feelings and to be able to call upon your Inner Guardian more quickly. This enables you to "feel" and read people more easily.

Any public place is a good spot to do this exercise. Busses and malls are great places to start. In time, you will find it easy to read people more accurately, to feel your way past the outer masks of people, and this will make you a more understanding person.

MALL
WATCHING

1. Go to a public spot and pick someone out of the crowd you can observe without being noticed.

2. Choose a stranger rather than a friend and begin with someone who appears to be the opposite of you.

The Empathic Reading (cont.)

3. **Imagine that you are that person.**

    Try to imagine that you are doing what that person would do. What is the person feeling? Can you predict how this person might act? What kind of day is this person having? What kind of life does this person have? What would it be like to be this person?

4. **In your Book of Enchantment, write down some of your impressions.**

    Include answers to the following statements:

    That kind of person must feel _____.

    If I were that person I would _____.

    I liked when that person _____.

    I was uncomfortable when that person _____.

VARIATION

Take a friend with you to this same place and choose a person to observe. Do not sit together as you observe, but do both observe the same person. Keep your observations 10 minutes or less so you do not intrude upon or make others uncomfortable. Then get together and compare notes. Discuss why you felt the things you felt about this person.

SUGGESTIONS FOR PARENTS

➤ **Explore some forms of healing touch with your young person.**

Take a class together. Learning healing touch is one of the best ways to develop and strengthen psychic ability. It also improves healing, balancing, and grounding for the individual at the same time.

➤ **Perform the psychic games with the young person in your life.**

This is especially effective with old family photograph albums. It provides opportunity to practice skill development, but it also provides opportunities to explore and share family history, strengthening the bonds between you.

➤ **Use the "Feeling the Aura" exercise to practice energy assessments on each other.**

This will help build stronger intimacy between you.

➤ Openly discuss times in which you have felt something only to discover that those feelings were correct. Also discuss the times in which you were wrong about what you felt.

Try to identify what was different about each of the times and what was the same. In this way you both learn to discern correct from incorrect feelings.

Lesson 4

Psychic Vision

I went blank and then I started seeing images.

I saw colors around him.

There were all of these strange images and forms.

I dreamt that this would happen.

I saw flashes of colors and twinkling lights that
came and went.

Seeing auras. Having visions. Dreaming the future. Gazing into crystal balls and magic mirrors. Seeing ghosts. There are so many different things associated with psychic vision. The traditional word for psychic sight, *clairvoyance*, literally means "clear seeing." It has become a catchall word for various types of psychic phenomena, ESP, and intuition, but there really are many different types of psychic vision. In this lesson, we will clarify some of the confusion surrounding these terms and show you simple and effective ways for awakening your own psychic vision.

Most people think of anything psychic as being a sixth sense, one in some way beyond the five senses of taste, touch, sight, hearing, and smell. What most

The All-Seeing Eye of Horus

Horus is one of the savior gods of the Egyptian tradition whose magic was always associated with artistic energies. Many believed that working with and praying to Horus would awaken vision and prophecy.

The Eye of Horus was a powerful symbol for protection and spiritual vision. During prayer and ritual, people wore or painted the image on their bodies when they were trying to foresee the future. Painting the symbol on the forehead or throat was believed to stimulate dreams which would reveal what was coming into your life or what was hidden from you.

people don't notice, though, is that when we first experience psychic phenomena, whichever of our usual five senses is the strongest will most likely become the way we experience the event. Some people are more visual than others, and for them psychic sight usually appears first. Some people are more auditory, so they usually begin having psychic experiences associated with hearing. Some people are more into their feelings, so psychic touch becomes the easiest way for them to begin developing their psychic abilities.

Unfortunately, what often happens is that those who have a strong sense of feeling wish they could develop their psychic abilities to see. Those who have a strong sense of hearing wish they could express their psychic abilities through feeling. And those who are best at seeing wish they could hear and feel. We never seem quite satisfied with the strengths we have. I guess this is what makes us human.

The truth is that all of our senses work together, but in the beginning, one or two may be a bit stronger and more sensitive. If we start by developing whichever sense is the strongest, the other psychic senses will come along in time. However, we must be patient and persist.

Most young people are *far* more psychic than adults are, often very naturally demonstrating and experiencing clairvoyant abilities. They see auras. They have prophetic dreams. They see spirit. They know when others are not being truthful, especially the adults around them. Many young people speak of the future and re-member past lives much more easily than adults. But like adults, young people don't know how to trust those experiences.

Believing is Seeing!

Expect to see and you do.

Expect to do and you will.

Psychic Vision Changes Our World

Psychic vision can be scary for everyone. The world is no longer just what we see and touch with our eyes and hands. Things are no longer black and white. There are subtleties at play around us all of the time. Psychic vision increases our awareness, changing the secure boundaries we have created around us. It prompts us to question things.

Have you ever seen pictures of horses pulling carriages and the horses have blinders on so they can focus only on what is directly in front of them? Most people go through life like this. Well, psychic vision removes those blinders. Suddenly we can see things happening beside us, behind us, and far into the distance.

The movies and television usually make psychic vision out to be very glamorous, something exciting and wonderful. AND IT IS! But with it comes new responsibilities. Sometimes you cannot control what you see, both the good and the bad. This is why learning to properly develop and control your psychic power is so very important.

About three months before my father died, I had a dream indicating I should visit him, so I arranged to spend a weekend with my parents. My father was feeling better and he even let me do some music therapy on him to ease the pain of the cancer that had moved into his back. As I worked on him, I saw a thick, black, tarlike substance spreading throughout his body. His cancer was growing worse and I saw why I had been prompted to visit him.

Later, after I returned home, I called him to ask if he would like me to do some long distance healing on him. He told me simply, "No, I don't think that will be necessary." As he said this to me, I had a flash of what was coming. He had made his decision to let go and I knew he would be gone before the year was out.

Over the next six to eight weeks his health declined rapidly. He passed away in early December, and although my psychic vision had pained me by revealing his coming death, it had also blessed me by nudging me to see him when we could both still enjoy seeing each other before his health took that final slide.

Two Forms of Psychic Vision

This dream encouraging me to visit my father and the flash during our phone conversation after the visit were both forms of psychic vision. What I saw physically when I performed the music therapy on him, his cancer actually spreading, was another form of psychic vision.

There are two forms of psychic vision, internal and external. Neither is any better nor worse than the other. They are just different.

Internal vision, or intuition, allows us to perceive things inside our mind. a bit like watching a movie. Sometimes an image comes to mind. Sometimes just a

What Clairvoyants Often See

OUTER VISION

People with psychic vision see many different kinds of things in their "outer" vision.

aura	the energy field around a person (colors and location tell much about a person's health and activities)
halos	part of the aura; a soft glow about the head and shoulders
changing images	faces and places change before eyes of person, reflecting changes, past or future, in people and places in person's life
future scenes	images and scenarios of the future, often seen as though happening presently
health problems	often seen on the person just as visibly as a bruise upon the skin would be
location imprints	events and people who have left strong imprints on places from the past.
persons who have passed over	family members and loved ones around themselves and others
objects appearing or disappearing	usually occurs when spirits are trying to get our attention
shadows and movements	often indicate presence of spirit or change in environment
spirit lights flickering	lights of various colors around someone, often indicating presence of spirit guides

thought passes through or nudges us. Sometimes we just get an impression or hunch that something is going to happen. Dreams are part of our internal vision.

With *external vision*, we see things with our physical eyes people usually don't see. Unlike internal vision, these things are not in our mind, but outside of us. We see the aura around a person. We see spirit faces behind us when we look into a mirror. We walk into a room and see shadows that would not normally be in the room, indicating something has happened here. With external vision, we see the spiritual and normally hidden aspects of life just as we see everything else in our world, and sometimes just as clearly as we see everything else.

A recent, very popular movie has a young boy who whispers to his therapist, "I see dead people." For this child, the outer vision, the physically seeing of things, was intrusive. This was just a story, but it shows how outer vision can become distracting. We do not want to be seeing things all of the time because it interferes with our regular life. If we were to be constantly bombarded with information, we would soon become overwhelmed with it all and not know what to do first.

The techniques and magical practices you will be learning in this book are very safe. They will help you to avoid the common problems of sensory overload, to eliminate your fears, and to understand your powers. Most of all, these activities will help you to control your powers so you can use them responsibly—when you wish and as much as you wish.

Types of Psychic Vision

There are four different kinds of psychic vision. These do overlap one another and there are variations in all of them. Most psychic vision experiences, though, will usually fall into one of these four categories. All four of them can show up as internal or external forms.

PRECOGNITION

Precognition, psychically knowing, seeing, or obtaining information about an event before it happens, can include different kinds of prophecy or just simple premonitions. Precognition is knowing the unknowable and seeing the unseen. It is knowing how something will happen at some time in the future, either the far or the near future.

Whenever important mail is coming my way, I will always dream of it a day or two beforehand. This is precognition. If you have had a hunch that something was going to happen and it did, you experienced precognition. If you just know that you were going to make your little brother eat a worm (well, O.K., that doesn't really apply here, but I think you get the idea). Precognition is knowing that something will happen in the future.

DISTANT VIEWING

Distant viewing, the ability to see people, places, and things from a great distance, takes a number of forms. *Telepathy* is the ability to send and receive messages over

Psychic Science

Past Life Visions

Reincarnation is the belief that after death we are reborn into another body. Each new body and new environment provides opportunity for our soul to learn and grow.

Have you been interested in a particular time in history?

Have you ever gone to a new place but it felt familiar?

Have you ever been particularly attracted to one culture?

Around the world millions of people believe in and have visions of past lives, times in which they have lived before. Scientists are continuing to investigate the spontaneous past life visions of young people. These are very common.

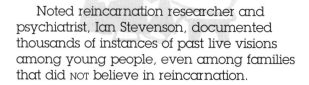

Noted reincarnation researcher and psychiatrist, Ian Stevenson, documented thousands of instances of past live visions among young people, even among families that did NOT believe in reincarnation.

So what did this show scientists?

The mind and body are connected. What happens on one level affects us on others. What happens at one time affects us in other times.

For scientists, psychologists and child therapists, this provides some possibilities for explaining childhood fears, possibly brought over from a previous life, and for understanding gifted abilities which may have developed in a previous life.

Past life visions offer opportunities for healing and exploring connections between the past and the present—and the present and the future.

Our ability to perceive is not limited by time or place.

WE CAN LOOK INTO
THE PAST OR ENVISION
THE FUTURE!

Learning to
trust our
impressions is
one of
the most
empowering
lessons in life.

a distance and falls into this category. We will explore telepathy in Lesson 6.

Another form of distant viewing is looking into the past, experiencing past life visions. With *astral travel* (also called out-of-body experiences), our consciousness or spirit leaves our body and travels to different places and times. *Long distance healing*, healing people from afar, is another form of distant viewing.

X-Ray Vision

X-ray vision is the ability to see inside of things. When I visited my father and saw the black substance spreading throughout his body, I physically saw it in his aura, but I also saw inside his body where I could see the cancer wrapping around his spine and several other parts of his body.

X-ray vision is most often used with healing, where it helps us direct our healing energies. Besides people, x-ray vision can be used to heal pets and other animals. It can also be used to look into the hidden aspects of events and people in our lives, seeing who or what is interfering or helping with our endeavors.

Spirit Vision

Ghosts of loved ones. Angels. Beings from the Faerie Realm. Hauntings. These kinds of *spirit vision* are the more popular forms of psychic power. Everyone, it seems, wants to see spirits. It's comforting to know we live on in some form after death. Unfortunately, what most people know about the spirit world and seeing spirits comes from the media and is almost always distorted or even entirely made up.

There are many aspects to the spirit world and to understanding our experiences with this realm. We will touch briefly on the basics and how to open up to the spirit world safely in the next lesson, Lesson 5.

There are, of course, other types of psychic experiences. In time, you will discover them. If you develop the basic skills, though, you will be equipped for both the usual and the unusual. You will learn how to trust your visions and your perceptions. You will find that any fears you have will be replaced with great wonder!

Beginning to Work with Psychic Vision

The best way to encourage your psychic vision is by developing your visualization skills. We explored the importance of visualizations in Volume I of this series, *Magic of Believing*. "The Magical Butterfly" visualization in that volume provides practice with stretching your imagination. This is especially helpful for those just beginning to work with their psychic vision. Visualization strengthens your internal vision and prepares the way for external vision.

You may also use some of the techniques for training and enhancing your internal vision shown in the table on the opposite page.

Practicing Visualization

Practice closing your eyes and visualizing objects around you in as much detail as possible. This lays a foundation for psychic vision.

➤ **Close your eyes and make a mental list of everything in your room and see in your mind's eye where these things are.**

Create a picture of your room in your mind.

➤ **Take time to regularly visualize the personal castle you created in the "Castle's Keep" magical practice from Volume I, *Magic of Believing*.**

Imagine all of its rooms and hallways. This also strengthens your memory and teaches you to pay attention to little things. Remember that our psychic messages often come quietly and subtly in the beginning.

➤ **Visualize the inside of yourself, creating an *inner smile*.**

Visualize each of your organs as happy and joyous. Creating a feeling of well being this way makes it easier for your psychic powers to come out.

➤ **Find a psychic friend or partner, someone you can trust.**

Practice scanning each other, imagining you have x-ray vision like. What can you see inside the other person?

Pay attention to everything that you feel and everything you imagine. Remember—imagining is a way of seeing.

Magical Practice

Psychic Vision Games

skills developed
- develops psychic abilities
- practices visualization
- provides fun and good times

There are many fun and simple ways to begin developing your psychic vision and many can be practiced anywhere, anytime. Use the simple practices here often in your daily life to awaken and keep your powers sharp.

Before playing any of these games, though, take a deep breath and relax. Clear your mind of all distractions and then focus on the particular situation. Imagine. Feel. Guess. You will be surprised how often you are correct.

Guess Who's on the Telephone

I love this one. It is easy to do and there are always lots of opportunities to practice it.

1. **The next time the phone rings, close yours eyes and try to "see" who is calling.**

   Trust your first impression (whoever or whatever pops into the mind).

2. **Whisper the name.**

   This teaches you to quickly use and trust your intuition. If nothing comes to mind, start with some quick questions, again trusting what comes to mind first. Is this person male or female? A relative? A friend?

3. **Partial answers do count.**

   Maybe, for example, you saw it was your mother calling. Instead, though, it was the neighbor woman or maybe your aunt. You still knew it was a female, and that is a great beginning.

SEEING THE UNSEEN

All these activities help develop x-ray vision, helping to move your internal vision to external vision.

✓ When you get a gift, try to envision what is inside.

✓ When someone comes to the door, try to "see" who before answering the door.

✓ In the morning before heading out to school, try to picture what your best friend or favorite teacher will be wearing.

Psych Out

Ring, Ring.
Who's there?
Alby.
Alby who?
Alby glad when I'm more psychic!

Magical Practice

Library of Answers

skills developed

- develops visualization
- brings greater clarity to psychic perceptions
- strengthens problem-solving ability

In the movie *Star Wars*, Luke Skywalker and his uncle purchase a couple of droids (robots), C3PO and R2D2. They take them home, clean them up, and check their programming so the droids will work for them. Often, our psychic powers are the same way. We have to get them out and clean them up now and then. We need to check their programming so they will work properly.

This exercise rings the doorbell of the closet where our psychic powers have been tucked away, waking them up and telling them to work for us in the way we want them to. It helps develop control of our psychic powers so we can easily use them in our everyday life.

In this exercise, we learn to envision a problem and then let our Inner Guardian bring us the answer. This way, we are using our psychic power to find possible solutions.

If you have read Volume I of this series, *Magic of Believing*, you know about the magical practice "Castle's Keep" in which you created your sacred castle, your safe haven for awakening your inner magic. For this exercise, we will use the Great Library in your castle.

I love books. Old books. New books. Dusty volumes. I like the feel of their weight in my hands. And I love what I can find in them. Because I love books, I also love libraries. They are one of my favorite places in the entire world. I've never met a library that I didn't like. I have seen some in small towns that are pretty pitiful and make my own collection of books seem magnificent, but I still love all libraries, big, little, and in between.

As a young person, libraries were my favorite place to spend time. I remember when my own local library limited how many books you could check out at one time. I was such a voracious reader I was given permission to take out as many books as I wanted at one time.

I learned early on what a great place a library is to find answers to questions and problems. Because of this, when I started creating my magical castle, the library was one of the first rooms I visualized in it. I made it the largest room in the castle, with books on every subject and for every problem.

In my castle library, books even speak to me. As I run my hands over their titles, they whisper me their contents. I even have a spirit guide who works as my librarian, helping me find answers to difficult problems. If I don't find what I'm looking for in my library, my librarian continues to look for me once I am gone.

Inevitably, within two to three days, the answer shows up somewhere in my life. I may come across the right book, see the exact information I need on television, or have a friend offer a solution. The next time I visit the library, I make a point of thanking my librarian spirit guide for her help.

As the years have passed, my library has taken on some modern conveniences. It now has a computer, television, movie screens and other wonders of modern technology. There is no limit to how you create your library. It's your castle. It's your haven.

Remember, in your library you are limited only by your own imagination.

Library of Answers (cont.)

ASK YOUR LIBRARIAN

- Create your sacred space.

- Perform a progressive relaxation.

1. **Bring to mind a problem that you are having.**

   It can be a worry or something you are concerned about. As you do, close your eyes.

2. **Visualize a door in front of you. See yourself standing and stepping through that doorway…**

You are standing in the great library. About you, from floor to ceiling, are bookshelves. Rows and rows of ancient and modern volumes. Here is all of the knowledge of the world. You reach out and softly touch the edges of several volumes. They each speak softly to you, enticing you to take them off the shelf, to read and learn.

As you look about, you remember the last time you were here. A volume had fallen off of the shelves, revealing a map of a secret passage. The passage lead to a special garden in which you saw a unicorn and found a hidden treasure (Volume 1, Magic of Believing, *"The Treasure Map" exercise*).

There is a soft noise behind you and you turn. There stands your librarian. The librarian smiles and asks, "May I help you find something?"

You blush a little, and then you softly tell the librarian what the problem or situation is. The librarian, nods, smiling knowingly and says, "Follow me. I think I know what you want."

Magical Practice

The librarian leads you through a maze of bookshelves, first turning one way, then another, and back again. You begin to wonder if the librarian knows where to go. It's almost as if the librarian is working through the maze of books as a way of working through the maze of your problem.

As you are wondering this, you almost walk into the back of the librarian, so caught up in your thoughts you did not realize the librarian had stopped in front of you.

Before you is a section of the library called, Problems and their Answers.

"I think this section will help. If you cannot find the answer here, I will continue to look for you. I should be able to find something you can use in a day or two."

The librarian smiles and disappears through the maze of bookshelves. You move to the first shelf and begin reading some of the titles:

Everything You Always Wanted to Know about Everything,

Everything You Always Wanted to Know about Nothing,

Answers to Questions Before They are Asked,

Riddle Me This; Answer Me That, *and*

Little Pogo Sticks: The Answer for Tired Grasshoppers.

There is an answer to everything!

As you look around you in this section, you realize the answer has to be here. You begin looking for it. You are amazed at how many books there are. It's as if for every possible problem or question, there is a book that has an answer.

Library of Answers (cont.)

"And if it's not here, I can find it for you."

You jump, startled. You did not hear the librarian return.

The librarian smiles and hands you a couple of books. "I think these will have the answers you seek."

You take them, and as you read the titles, they apply specifically to your problem.

Again, the librarian smiles and turns to walk back through the maze of shelves. You follow. Soon you are standing before the door through which you came in from.

As always, you are filled with amazement. "Thank you," you say to the librarian, who smiles warmly and turns to attend to the books.

You step back through the doorway into your sacred space and your room, bringing the answers with you. You are filled with confidence. There is no doubt that you will see the answers—and soon.

- **Perform a grounding ritual.**

Take time to record the experience in your Book of Enchantment. Watch what happens in the next day or two. Your answer will come to you. It may come as an inspiration, as advice from a friend, or even in the from of a dream, but it will come. You will see and know what to do.

Magical Practice

Library of Answers (cont.)

VARIATIONS

✓ Have a television room in the castle and as you change the channels, answers to different problems occur.

✓ Visualize a large movie screen or chalkboard where you can see the problem pictured or written out.

See the problem disappear by being erased. Sometimes the erasing is all that is necessary to help the problem be solved.

At other times, visualize and imagine the solution magically appearing on the screen or chalkboard after erasing the problem. In time, this exercise can become quite effective.

The asking
of the
question
is the
beginning of
the answer!

Crystal Gazing

SKILLS DEVELOPED	• **develops visualization skills** • **strengthens psychic vision** • **enhances creative imagination** • **sharpens divination ability**

We've all seen images of a gypsy woman sitting before a crystal ball, gazing deeply into it. She speaks softly and hauntingly of what she sees, describing it to the person sitting across from her. *Crystal gazing* and *scrying*, making out something that is unclear by looking carefully, are some of the most ancient tools of psychic vision. Crystal gazing practitioners were found throughout Mesopotamia and among the Druids and other peoples of Europe and China.

By crystal gazing, I mean using different types of the mineral quartz. Although glass lead crystal is used for gazing, it is not nearly as effective as natural quartz crystal and is much more difficult to work with. Quartz crystals emit a form of electrical energy that helps stimulate our natural psychic powers.

SELECTING YOUR CRYSTAL

In modern times, quartz crystals have grown quite popular. No New Age store is without its supply of various crystals and stones. Quartz crystals can be found in many sizes and shapes. Although most people associate crystal balls with psychic vision, the shape of the quartz crystal does not matter. I recommend you have one that fits into your hand.

Your quartz crystal point should be at least three inches long and at least an inch and a half thick. If you are using a crystal ball, it should be no less than two to three inches in diameter. Crystal points are much less expensive than crystal balls and just as effective.

The crystal you choose does not need to be perfectly clear. In fact, in the beginning it is better if the crystal has natural formations, cloudiness, and patterns. These markings make it easier to see things in the crystals.

In Lesson 2, we learned how to do cloud readings, seeing shapes in the clouds which have meaning for us. In beginning crystal gazing, looking for images in the crystal's natural formations is a similar kind of pattern recognition process. It is the best way to start to learn gazing. Just as with cloud reading, your Inner Guardian will help you to see those things in the crystal formations that apply to you or the question.

Magical Practice

CARE OF YOUR CRYSTAL

Your gazing crystal should only be used for this purpose. Always physically clean the crystal before and after each use. Mild soap and water is all that is necessary.

Energize your crystal periodically. About once a month, set it outside in the sunlight and moonlight for 24 to 36 hours.

Let others handle your gazing crystal only if you are gazing for them. When not using your crystal, keep it wrapped in a silk cloth to protect it. Silk is protective and prevents accidental imprinting from other people in the environment.

Crystal Gazing (cont.)

PERFORMING A SIMPLE
CRYSTAL GAZING

- **Create your sacred space.**

- **Perform a progressive relaxation.**

1. **Holding your crystal in your hands, begin slow, rhythmic breathing. Focus on what the problem is or on what you wish to know about.**

   Sometimes it is helpful to say a prayer or affirmation. This signals your Inner Guardian you would like help.

2. **As you hold the crystal, feel it coming to life. Imagine the electrical energy within it growing stronger, helping to stimulate your psychic vision.**

   Some people like to stroke the crystal softly to help awaken its energy. It is kind of like turning on the power just like you would flip on a light.

3. **Hold the crystal so you can look upon it easily.**

   Do not stare intently at it. Just look at the crystal with a soft gaze. It is the kind of stare you would have if you were looking off, daydreaming.

   Stay relaxed, and as you look into the crystal, pay attention to its formations.

Magical Practice

4. **Turn your crystal slowly in your hand so you can see how the light plays through the crystal in different ways.**

   You will see different forms as you rotate your crystal. Your Inner Guardian will help you to recognize images in the formations of the crystal that relate to your questions, as with the cloud readings.

5. **As you gaze at the crystal, watching the forms change, ask yourself some questions.**

   What does that image mean to me?

   Is it positive or negative?

   What else could it mean?

6. **Pay attention to any emotions you feel and trust them.**

   Remember, you will see and feel what your Inner Guardian knows you can relate to and what relates to your question or concern.

* **Perform a grounding ritual.**

RECORD YOUR RESPONSES IN YOUR
BOOK OF ENCHANTMENT.

Crystal Gazing (cont.)

With every crystal gazing, you strengthen your ability to work with your Inner Guardian. You increase the development of your psychic power. Crystals are tools with which you can build great levels of psychic power.

In time, the images you see will shift and become clearer. You will see clouds appearing and disappearing. Eventually, very detailed scenarios will start to appear in your gazing crystal, leading to great psychic vision into the future.

SUGGESTIONS FOR PARENTS

➤ **Young people who see and know things often feel different.**

These young people can often be loners and feel out of place. Without pushing your young people to develop psychic potentials, simply acknowledge the experiences, treating them as normal. This can be one of the best gifts you can give the young people in your life.

Share with the young people in your life times in which you have experienced "seeing" or "knowing." It will make them feel more secure in sharing their visionary experiences with you.

➤ **Go shopping together to find your own quartz gazing stones and crystal balls.**

➤ **Begin sharing dreams and discussing what they might mean.**

Look for recurring symbols and create your own personal dictionary of images.

➤ **Take an art or creative writing class together.**

These are wonderful and somewhat "normal" ways to stimulate the imagination and our visionary abilities, psychic or otherwise.

➤ **Practice some of the "Psychic Vision Games" from this lesson with the young persons in your life.**

These games can encourages them and will very likely surprise you as well.

Lesson 5

What About Ghosts?

So who am I likely to meet in the spirit realm?

Will I meet my guardian angel?

Will I get to find out if fairies and elves are real?

Do those animals that appear to me at special and important times in my life mean anything?

I imagine most of you are pretty excited about this chapter. Ghosts and spirits are fun stuff. Some of you may even be a little fearful. Whatever you are feeling or believing is O.K. By the time we finish this lesson, you will have a much better understanding of the spirit world—and a lot less fear.

No area of the psychic world gets as much attention as ghosts and spirits. What's more, it's the one area most often misunderstood. You need to become comfortable with the spirit world because as you awaken your psychic powers, you will be having contact with spirit at some time. You *will* have encounters with the spirit world. The best thing to do, then, is to learn more about the spirit realm and become comfortable and practiced at handling encounters easily.

The Great Gifts of Spirit Contact

*Our spirit guides encourage, prompt,
heal, protect, and enlighten us throughout
our daily lives—often without our realizing it.*

- Loved ones from our past comfort us.

- Angelic presence protects us.

- The Faerie Realm brings us great wonder.

- The ancient masters come to guide, teach, and mystify us.

- Guiding spirits serve as muses for inspiring our creativity.

- The medicine of spirit animal totems empower us.

First of all, forget everything you have seen on television or in movies. Experiences with spirit are not limited to seance rooms, old castles, or times past. Many people have had some experience with spirit phenomena. Something will be seen when nothing is there. A voice will be heard when no one else is present. There's a feeling of someone standing behind or beside us. The face of a special grandparent who has passed on years ago may be seen in a mirror or in a recent photograph.

So let's begin by getting rid of the misconceptions and by easing your fears. When you release your fears of the spirit world, you will be in a position to benefit the most from contact with it. You will be able to appreciate these experiences with a greater sense of wonder and possibility.

The Reality of Spirits and Spooks

When it comes to the reality of spirits, most people fall into one of several categories. Some believe that all spirit contact should be avoided and is nothing more than a doorway to evil. Others believe there is absolutely nothing to fear about the spirit world because as long as they maintain positive thoughts and a white light, nothing can ever harm them. The truth, as with most things, falls somewhere in between.

Over the years, a lot of nonsense has been promoted about the spirit world. Most of it makes for good stories, but it has nothing to do with the reality of it all. As long as we use a little common sense, there is nothing to

Psych Out

GHOSTLY
MADNESS

What do you call it when a ghost makes
mistakes?
A boo-boo!

What did the father ghost tell the little
ghost?
Don't spook until you're spooken to.

Why didn't the spirit buy a lottery ticket?
He didn't think he had a ghost of a chance.

What do ghosts ride at the amusement park?
The roller ghoster.

What did Mama Ghost say to Baby Ghost
before taking off?
Fasten your sheet belt.

If people keep canaries as pets, what do
ghosts keep?
Boo-jays.

Why is fall the favorite season of ghosts?
Because that's when haunting season opens.

worry about when working with the spirit world. We can eliminate most of the fears and problems surrounding any contact with the spirit realm by remembering three things:

THERE ARE ALL KINDS OF SPIRITS

Most of what you see on television or in the movies about the spirit world is pure fabrication. The media wants to sell products or tickets. Some people enjoy going to the movies just to be scared. Yes, being scared can be fun at times. However, don't confuse the spirit world portrayed in horror movies with the real thing.

There are as many different kinds of spirits as there are people. They have their own tasks and lives to lead. Many of them serve as helpers and guides to loved ones still alive. Others are learning and growing in the spirit world itself. Some are preparing to be reborn into the physical. Others have tasks that have nothing to do with us directly and we probably would not understand what's going on anyway.

In truth, there is more we don't know about the spirit world than we do. It is still a relatively uncharted land, but this book will prepare you for your adventures in the spirit world and provide you with safe tools for exploring spirit. This is, after all, an advantage most adults, including many of your parents, have not had. You are the young explorers, the adventurers into new realms.

The spirit world is not a place of heaven or hell. It has many layers, many neighborhoods, all with their own unique qualities. Think of the spirit world as a foreign country. It has it's own customs. It has its own rules. It has its own language. You can get the most benefit from visiting a foreign country if you take the time to learn how to communicate and act properly with the people there. The more you learn about the country, the more enjoyable your visit will be.

YOUNG PEOPLE HAVE NATURAL PSYCHIC ABILITIES

Young people today are so much more capable and much more knowledgeable than the youth of even a generation ago. Most of the time, spirit can communicate with you more easily than adults, whether through inspiration, dreams, conversations in your sacred space, or even through actual appearances.

Caution...

You do not need a "trance ticket" to visit the spirit world. **Trance work creates physical and emotional health problems. In fact, it is particularly problematic for young people. Forget what you may have heard or seen about trance.** Today trance is unnecessary. We know more and can communicate with spirit very easily without it.

There are still those who believe the best way to communicate with spirit is through a *trance*, becoming unconsious to allow spirits to speak through you. This is simply not true. In fact, trance work is fraught with problems, including physical and emotional ones. Many believe it's a quick and easy way to communicate with spirit, which is unfortunately why it remains popular, but the problems associated with trance far outweigh any of the benefits.

Trance work has served its purpose and was good for what people knew at the time. Today there are safer and more effective techniques for opening to the spirit world without also taking on the problems associated with this form of communication with spirit.

Young people today have come into this world with stronger abilities and greater opportunities to communicate with spirit naturally and safely. The intent of this book, indeed the entire Young People's School of Magic and Mystery series, is to empower you so avoid the mistakes others have made in creating the magical life.

You Control Your Contact with Spirit

The spirit world can be a wonderful place to get enlightenment and guidance. It is a great place to visit, but it is not a place to escape our daily lives. You will not have to worry about such things as possession and attack, anymore than you would worry about the tourist bureau of a foreign country kidnapping you or taking you hostage—if you approach the spirit world with common sense.

About Working with Spirits

➤ **You should always control all aspects of work with spirits.**

If a spirit displays a behavior you do not like, dismiss it immediately. It does not take anything more than a strong voice and attitude. Your true spirit guides will not say or do things to make you uncomfortable.

➤ **If something the spirit does or says makes you uncomfortable, honor that feeling!**

➤ **Your spirit guides are there to guide—not to do for you.**

➤ **Spirit guides do not necessarily know what's best.**

There is growing and learning in the spirit realm as there is in ours. Just because a loved one or guide is in spirit does not mean the entity is automatically wiser and knows what's best for us. Different spirits have different abilities, just as different people have different abilities.

➤ **You must test spirits.**

Never accept what they say blindly. Make them prove themselves to you again and again. Our true spirit guides know we need to do this and they will not be hurt or offended because we are testing them. If they do seem to get upset with your testing, they are not your true guides.

The key to preventing all troubles with spirit is remembering that you must control all work with this realm. You are in charge. If an entity demonstrates a quality that makes you feel uncomfortable or a behavior that is inappropriate, you must dismiss it firmly. Tell that entity to go home! If we invited someone into our home and that individual spilled things or otherwise behaved inappropriately, you would tell that person to leave and not invite them back again. The same is true for spirits.

If we tell the spirit to leave in a strong, firm, and clear voice, it will do so. On rare occasions, we may have to repeat it, but 99 percent of all problems with spirit arise when people do not assert their control over the situation. They mistakenly believe that spirit is more powerful or evolved simply because it is no longer physical. This simply is not true.

If any spirit displays a quality or temperament that you do not like, dismiss it. We do not have to put up with stupid behavior in our normal relationships and we do not have to tolerate it in our spiritual relationships either. If a spirit makes you feel uncomfortable, **honor** that feeling and dismiss the spirit immediately.

Doubts and worries will not offend your true guides. If a spirit displays impatience, recognize that as a sign something is wrong. Dismiss the spirit because it obviously does not have your best interest at heart. Your true spirit guides are not going to make you feel uncomfortable.

Psychic Absurdicus

Fun, Absurd, and Strange
Psychic Practices

GHOST IN
THE GRAVEYARD

On warm summer nights, my brothers and our friends loved to play Ghost in the Graveyard, a spooky form of tag. We didn't realize, though, that this game had some very strange origins.

Most ghost stories center around the *bogie man*, a term that now applies to any tormenting or frightening spirit. In parts of Europe long ago, one such bogie man was the *ankou*.

The ankou was the graveyard watcher. When a new graveyard was built, it was customary to bury someone alive in the first grave. In this way a ghostly guardian or graveyard watcher was created.

This tormented soul would frighten off others—alive or dead—so that the peace of the departed would not be disturbed.

Kinds of Spirit Guides

Every society had its own way of classifying and naming spirits and ghosts. In reality, there are as many different kinds of spirit beings and guides as there are people. Some will be guardians. Some will help with healing. Some are teachers, and some are loving companions. However, four types are the most common spirit beings encountered.

SPIRITS, APPARITIONS, AND GHOSTS

A *spirit* is any being or entity that lives, works, and operates on a non-physical level. It is a general term, often interchanged with ghost and some of the other terms described here. It can be used to refer to angels, guides, beings of nature, and souls of those departed from physical life.

An *apparition* is any object, being, or place of supernatural origin and if often used interchangeably with the term ghost.

Supernatural, for now, refers to anything we do not have a direct scientific explanation for. It is a visual experience. Although it is often the vision of someone long deceased, it can also be the vision of an object, an animal such as a deceased pet, or even a particular place. The word implies the return of someone after death to familiar surroundings, usually to accomplish a particular goal.

Sometimes this is unfinished business and objects and places appearing as apparitions may reflect something unresolved.

Ghost and *discarnate* are terms applied to the spirit of a person who has died and usually this spirit is visible. For our purposes, we will use it to represent any spirit of someone who is no longer alive.

Most people at some time or other have had an experience with ghosts, generally with a loved one who has passed on. Although this can be unsettling, it is not something to be feared. It should be embraced as a wonderful gift. It affirms for us that we are never truly separated from those we love. They do not stop loving us after death. Their spirits commonly remain or return briefly to confirm this for us. Many times spirits of family members may remain close to serve as guides and guardians to those left behind. They are usually recognized through familiar touches, smells, and even actual appearances.

Although startling, this is not an experience to be feared or shied away from. Instead, we should try to become comfortable with these kinds of appearances and embrace them with joy.

Psych Out

Eenie Meenie,
Chile beanie—
The spirits are
about to speak...

Bullwinkle J. Moose

ANGELS AND SPIRIT GUIDES

Angels are a part of most major religions in the Western hemisphere and appear in all religions and all literature throughout the world. In the past decade, angels have become quite popular, even among traditional religions and churches. This interest has served to create a bridge for people to the possibility of other dimensions.

What is often called an angel may be nothing more than some other kind of spirit guide. Spirits of family members who still watch over us are often called angels. Spirit beings assisting us in some way are often called angels. The word *angel* means "message," and thus any spirit being that brings us a message is technically an angel. For our purposes, though, we will distinguish angels from other types of spirit beings by defining angels as a separate line of life who have not lived in human form but have bodies of lighter substance (often invisible to us) and embody a creative and loving intellect.

A *spirit guide* is any spirit being serving as a guide or protector for us. Often the term means any spirit who assists. Spirit guides serve a multitude of functions and we can have a variety of guides helping us throughout our lives. A spirit guide may take a variety of forms, whether a favorite relative watching over us, the shape of an animal reflecting the guide's qualities and characteristics, or geometric shapes or different colors which symbolize its energy. Whatever the spirit guide's form, we

Testing Your Guides

We are human and have doubts. We need assurances and confirmation from our spirit guides. The most important way to learn to trust our guides is by testing them. I have guides I have been working with since I was a child, and I still test them. This will not offend your true spirit guides.

Keep in mind that tests should be reasonable and doable within a relatively short amount of time, from a few days to a week. Relationships require work, so always test several times. Remember, though, not everything can be assisted by spirit. Consider asking you guides for help with the following things:

➤ finding you good parking spots,

➤ giving you answers through your dreams,

➤ showing themselves in your dreams,

➤ helping you find good tickets for events,

➤ providing favors,

➤ helping smooth out rough situations,

➤ sending you helpful messages for your friends (keep in mind they will not give you gossip on friends),

➤ placing opportunities in your path,

➤ providing guidance and solutions to problems, and

➤ helping boost your psychic power so you may recognize it more easily.

need to study its symbolism to understand the role the guide is serving in our life.

Guides will often communicate to us through our strongest sense or through the sense that will help us to recognize the communication most easily. Rarely have I ever seen my grandfather in a human form since he passed away. However, he smoked Camel unfiltered cigarettes his entire life and when he shows up in spirit, it is always with the smell and appearance of the smoke I associated with him throughout my childhood. After his visit, my clothes and surroundings will continue to smell of smoke.

Spirit guides do not always know best for us—death does not necessarily make us any wiser

Inviting Nature
Spirit Encounters

➤ **Spend time in nature.**

You cannot expect to encounter nature spirits if you do not spend time where they are found.

➤ **Meditate and pray regularly in Nature.**

This can be under trees, next to ponds or at creek beds, and at the seashore.

➤ **Take up a fun, creative activity.**

Nature spirits are drawn to anyone who expresses joy at doing something, even if they aren't very good at it.

➤ **Let an area of your yard grow wild so nature spirits have a place to play.**

➤ **Sing often and learn to play something musical even if you aren't very good at it.**

Nature spirits are drawn to those who try to express themselves through music.

➤ **Be loving, appreciative, and protective of all things in nature.**

NATURE SPIRITS

Nature spirits are those beings associated specifically with nature. Every society taught there were spirits associated with everything growing upon the planet and every tradition had its own way of naming them. In the Western world, we most often refer to them as fairies and elves, but they have many other names.

Nature spirits are Mother Earth's children. They are as many sided as nature itself, coming in a multitude of sizes, forms, and degrees of development and creativity. Every flower has its fairy, every tree its spirit. There are unicorns and other fantastic creatures within the natural world as well.

Most people have had contact with this realm without ever realizing it. If you've ever seen flashes of light around plants and flowers, you have probably encountered a flower spirit. If you've ever caught the fragrance of a flower or tree as you walked by, you received a greeting from its spirit. Most children's imaginary friends are not imaginary at all but often part of this group.

Nature spirits have many magical abilities and can teach us much. They are masters of glamour, which we explored in Volume I of this series. They hold the secrets of shape-shifting. They inspire creativity. They are the keepers of the Earth's treasures. They hold the keys to all of the mysteries of nature, healing and otherwise.

Signs of Spirit

Sense	Common Spirit Phenomena
SEEING (clairvoyance)	shadows and movements out of the corner of the eyes; faces and forms in mirrors, doorways, or windows; flickering lights of different colors; objects being moved or disappearing and reappearing.
HEARING (clairaudience)	whispers behind you when no one is present; hearing our name called; house settling noises when it is not; music and singing from unidentified sources (especially when out in nature); ringing, buzzing, and popping in the ears.
FEELING (clairsentience)	chills and goose bumps; changes in temperature; the fly-walking-through-the-hair feeling; adrenaline rushes; feeling of a spider web brushing over the face when none is present; changes in the air pressure around you; lightheadedness.
SMELLING (clairfragrant)	whiffs of flowers and plants when none are around; fragrances associated with those who are no longer alive and from which the source is unidentifiable.
TASTING (clairgustus)	sweet or sour tastes in the mouth (not associated with eating or belching); tastes associated with one who is no longer alive (that is, someone associated with a particular dish).

Spirit Animals and Totems

Many traditions taught there are animals that reflect our spirit. Animals that appear in dreams, in times of trouble, in unusual ways, and in our lives repeatedly serve as messengers for us. They are often referred to as animal *totems* or *spirit animals*.

Sometimes in meditation, our spirit guides will show themselves not as a person, but as an animal. By studying the animal, we can understand the role of that spirit guide in our life.

One of the ways the nature spirits speak to us is through the animals that appear in our life. To begin identifying your animal guides, ask yourself the following:

Do you dream of certain animals regularly?

Have you had unusual experiences with certain animals?

Are there certain animals that you have always been drawn to?

Are there certain animals you are afraid of?

What animal do you see more often than your friends do?

If you were an animal, which one would you like to be?

Hauntings

Ghosts are found to exist around the world. Yes, traditional ghosts may be found in old homes, but in this country they are also found in southern mansions, modern two-story homes, apartments, and other dwellings. There are homes with footsteps echoing, doors opening and closing on their own, and furniture being rearranged. Sometimes the ghost appears as an apparition or as simply a dark shape. On other occasions, a voice is heard uttering groans or fragrances are smelled.

There are many strange phenomena in the world. Some, if examined closely, have valid explanations. Others, even after careful examination, still go unexplained. Those with no obvious cause remain so primarily for two reasons. There may be a lack of evidence and understanding. Or emotions, usually fear, contribute to distortion of the events involved.

True spirit phenomena, even if strange, are not necessarily negative forces at work or a haunting. Usually spirit tries to get our attention softly. If we are not listening, the knock on our doors of attention may get louder. Just the same, it is always important not to jump to conclusions or to make assumptions.

COMMON MISUNDERSTANDINGS
ABOUT HAUNTINGS

Disturbances, poltergeists, and possession are often the stuff of movies and as a result, suffer from some common misconceptions.

DISTURBANCES

Disturbances are unusual experiences without any valid explanation. These can range from knocks and sounds in the night to people breaking out in chills and goosebumps in one area of a home. These experiences are not harmful in any way. They are only disturbing in the same way that your brother or sister's bad habits can be irritating. The events can, in fact, be amusing and provide for some good conversation.

When we start awakening our psychic powers, we become more sensitive to subtle things going on around us. Many disturbances may well have always gone on around us, but we did not sense them because we were ignoring our psychic perceptions. Sometimes disturbances can simply be a spirit guide trying to get our attention.

It's not a good idea, however, to invite disturbances. I know it seems like fun at parties to play with a Quija board or hold mock seances, but this kind of activity can become troublesome if you don't know what you are doing. We've all seen movies where someone has a party and all of sudden uninvited guests show up. The person holding the gathering starts running around trying to keep everything under control, but everything gets out of hand. This is what often happens when Quija boards are used or seances held without proper training. Spirit guests show up you wouldn't normally invite into your home.

Caution...

Be aware that just reading the directions on a Quija board game does not mean you know what you are doing. The Quija board can open doorways to disturbances by amplifying hidden emotional and psychic energies in those participating and this creates a doorway for uninvited spirit guests.

POLTERGEIST

Poltergeist literally means "noisy ghost" and refers to activities of spirit which are not just disturbing, but usually distressful. It can be something as simple as unexplained noises such as simple pops and cracks, or it can be as intense as things in the home actually breaking.

There has often been great debate as to the true existence of poltergeists. This kind of activity often occurs in homes where there are adolescent children or children going through puberty, especially girls. One theory suggests that as the young person enters puberty, a tremendous amount of psychic energy (corresponding to awakening sexual energies) is released in an uncontrolled manner, resulting in erratic expression of these energies in strange phenomena.

The human body is a bio-chemical, electro-magnetic energy system. Our sexual energy is linked to our electrical aspects. As the sexual energy increases, so does our own electrical frequency. Poltergeist activity may be like an electrical short, giving off uncontrolled sparks.

Most poltergeist phenomena are eliminated through balancing the psychic energies and finding creative outlets for the newly awakened sexual energy of puberty. That certainly includes avoiding dabbling in psychic activities such as trances, seances, or Quija board games without learning proper techniques.

POSSESSION

Although many cases of possession have been reported and are often the subject of talk shows, I have never personally encountered a true case of possession. I have been consulted and helped investigate a number of possession cases around the country, but I have yet to experience a legitimate case. As long as we lead a balanced, healthy life, we will **never** have to worry over any such thing even if we are working with spirit.

Spectres and Hauntings

Most of what people know and believe about hauntings is from fictional accounts on television, in movies, and in books. People like to be scared and such stories sell by playing upon people's fears—even if the tales are untrue.

The entertainment industry likes to tap into the primal fears of parents, so often fosters a belief that children and young people are more susceptible to possession and attacks by spirit. **This perception is false!**

Even though children and young adults are generally more perceptive of the spirit realm than adults, they have an extremely protective energy and a strong light surrounding them. As long as anyone, young people or adults, stay healthy, balanced, and use common sense, they will never experience anything like possession.

Spirit guides will
always
help us—
but not "do"
for us.

Magical Practice

Calling Upon Guardian Angels

skills developed
- protects all psychic and spirit activities
- strengthens spirit contact

An old legend tells of a group of angels that watch over us when we are born. They stay with us through our life until we step out and follow our own spiritual and magical path. At that time, one angel from that group steps forward and serves as our Holy Guardian Angel.

Working with angels is one of the safest ways for you to begin your work with the spirit realm. By opening to them first, you can then have the angels protect you in all of your psychic, magical, and spiritual work. They strengthen and protect your sacred space. They help you in working on your psychic development as well as in working with all of your spirit guides.

In Lesson 1, you learned how to create your sacred space. As you become used to entering your sacred space and comfortable with the process, you will be able to add special practices to strengthen the experience. In this magical practice, you will call upon the four great archangels to bring protection to your sacred space and your psychic activities there.

THE FOUR GREAT ARCHANGELS

- Set the mood.

- Perform a relaxation   technique.

1. Enter your sacred space.

2. Practice saying the names of the archangels until you are comfortable with the pronunciations.

   You will be most effective in calling upon the four great archangels by pronouncing each of their names properly, with three syllables.

   The names should be pronounced slowly and with three syllables each. Three is a creative and magical number. Each syllable gets equal emphasis.

Raphael	say	*Rah-fah-ehl*
Gabriel	say	*Gah-bree-ehl*
Michael	say	*Me-kah-ehl*
Auriel	say	*Ah-ree-ehl*

3. **When you are comfortable with the pronunciation of the archangel names, try adding toning to the pronunciation of the names.**

    Magical toning heightens the effect of the proper pronunciation. Magical toning has been used in all traditions around the world to give power to prayers and invocations.

    Toning is the pronunciation of words with a special kind of breathing. As you inhale, say the archangel name silently. As you exhale, say the same archangel name audibly. Practice this until you are comfortable with it.

4. **Once you have become comfortable with toning, practice the following little prayer, combining calling the four archangels to surround you with toning.**

    On your breath in, say the first line silently. On your breath out, say the same first line audibly. Then move on to the next line, toning each line as you recite the magical invocation.

    Raphael in front of me.

    Gabriel behind me.

    Michael to the right of me.

    Auriel to the left of me.

    Angels surround, bless, and protect me.

Calling Upon Guardian Angels (cont.)

•   **Perform a grounding ritual**

This magical invocation can be used to help you dismiss any spirits that make you uncomfortable. It is also a very good prayer to begin and end your visits to your sacred space or begin and end your magical practices.

Magical Practice

Archangel

ARCHANGEL	DIRECTION	SEASON
RAPHAEL	East	SPRING SEASON: the angel of beauty, brightness, and healing
GABRIEL	West	WINTER SEASON: angel of love and hope
MICHAEL	South	AUTUMN SEASON: angel of strength, balance, and protection
AURIEL	North	SUMMER SEASON: angel of great vision and creative abundance

Calling Upon Guardian Angels (cont.)

Symbolism

SYMBOL	COLOR	GIFT
sun	blue and gold	bringer of miracles and guardian of sacred quests
lily; white rose	emerald green	strengthens our perceptions and guards the sacred places upon the Earth, including your own sacred space
flaming sword	reds and russets of fall season	brings control, balance, and illumination to our psychic activities
green vines and fruit	brilliant white (sometimes black and yellow)	opens us to the Faerie Realm and the blessings of Nature

Magical Practice

Inviting Angels and Spirit Guides

skills developed
- increases spirit guide contact
- initiates contact with angels

When we work to meet our spirit guides, it is important we are consistent and set up a safe place for them as well. This is why creating the sacred space and the calling of the archangels is so important. This magical practice builds upon your ability to create sacred space by increasing your safety liklihood of success in your efforts.

With practice, you will be able to invite the angels and other guides into your sacred space and into your life with great success. In the beginning, though, do not get discouraged if your spirit guide does not appear in any way that you can readily detect. Thank the spirit anyway.

Courtesy is as important when working with spirit beings as it is with human beings. Even if you can't detect the spirit guide, that doesn't mean it's not there. You simply may not be able to tune in effectively yet.

Have a Conversation with Your Guide

- **Set the mood.**

- **Perform a relaxation technique.**

1. **Create your sacred space and call to the archangels so you will be protected in your efforts.**

    Imagine and feel them around you, protecting you. Remember, as we learned in Volume I of this series, all energy follows our thoughts. So even if you don't feel them, imagining them there is the important thing. It opens the bridge to allow them into your sacred space.

2. **See a doorway opening before you and step through it into a sacred place within your inner castle.**

    This can be a chapel, an outdoor garden, or temple area on the castle grounds—any place that is a sanctuary for you. Use your imagination. Know that in this place the spirit world and the human world can come together.

    I like to have spirit show themselves as apparitions and then solidify into real people in the midst of an outdoor temple. Some people like to have lovely outdoor gardens with of the paths leading to a special spot where spirit comes to visit. Some people have rooms with doors and a knock on the other side signals a spirit guide. Find what works best for you.

Magical Practice

3. **In your mind, begin to carry on a conversation with this being.**

   Pay attention to everything that you experience. Ask the guide questions:

   What is its purpose?

   Why is it around you?

   How can you recognize its presence in your daily life?

   Are there things it will do to let you know it is

   around?

   Is there something important that you need to know?

   Do not force the answers. Let them come naturally. Do not worry that you are simply imagining it all. You would not be able to imagine it if there wasn't some reality to it.

4. **Ask the spirit guide for some sign in the next week so you can verify its reality.**

   Is there something coming that you should know about? Ask for a specific physical sensation to occur to you often in the next week to know the presence of this spirit guide.

Inviting Angels and Spirit Guides (cont.)

5. Thank the spirit guide for the opportunity to meet and work with it.

6. Breathe deeply, relaxing, and repeat the angelic prayer of protection.

   As you do, see and feel yourself back within your own sacred space.

• Perform a grounding ritual.

Magical Practice

VARIATION FOR MORE PERSONAL CONTACT WITH AN ARCHANGEL

- Set the mood.

- Perform a relaxation technique.

1. Create your magic space.

2. Awaken it and strengthen it through the angelic prayer of the previous magical practice.

3. As you relax, step through the doorway into the sanctuary of the inner castle.

4. Call specifically to one of the archangels to come and visit you.

   Magically tone the name of the archangel three times. (For example, Gabriel, Gabriel, Gabriel.).

5. Visualize and imagine a large crystalline bubble of the angel's color drifting toward you and coming into your castle sanctuary.

Inviting Angels and Spirit Guides (cont.)

6. **Out of this bubble, visualize the great archangel stepping out to speak to you.**

   Carry on a conversation in your head.

7. **At the end, imagine the archangel stepping forward and embracing you.**

   You feel yourself lighter, healed and blessed. Before the embrace is broken, the angel whispers a promise into your ear

8. **Thank the archangel and allow this wonderful being to step back into that bubble and drift back into the spirit world—until you call upon it again.**

• **Perform a grounding technique.**

Magical Practice

Smoke and Fire Readings

skills developed

- makes discovery of spirit guides easier
- strengthens ability to work with symbols and images
- enhances psychic ability

This is one of my favorite psychic activities. It always works and it can be great fun.

HOWEVER, CERTAIN PRECAUTIONS ARE ABSOLUTELY REQUIRED (see *Cassandra Says...* on the opposite page).

In preparation for this exercise, gather together the following items:

✓ galvanized tub or fireproof container (18 to 24 inches in diameter) with several inches of sand in the bottom,

✓ candle at least six inches tall and matches,

✓ pack of parchment paper,

   Regular paper will do, but parchment works better. It has an oil in it that helps the smoke to run. Experiment with different papers.

✓ pair of tweezers or tongs, and

✓ small bucket of water.
   This is to drop any paper in that might catch fire.

Caution...

✓ An older person or an adult figure should supervise this magical practice as it involves the use of lit candles and paper.

✓ Follow all preparations **carefully** to prevent the possibility of fire.

✓ Do **not** perform this practice inside the home or near anything flammable.

SMOKE SIGNALS

• **Set the mood.**

1. **Create your sacred space, including calling upon the angels to surround you and protect you.**

2. **Charge a piece of paper with your energy and intentions.**

   Write your name and birth date on one side of the paper.

   Hold the paper against your solar plexus with both hands and begin deep, slow breathing. Inhale for a count of four, hold for a count of four, and exhale for a count of four.

   As you exhale, visualize the paper being charged with your energy and your intention to find out whom you spirit guides are.

   You have "charged the paper," imprinting it with your energy and your intention.

2. **Invite your spirit guides into your sacred space.**

   After several minutes, close your eyes and begin a progressive relaxation. Send warm soothing thoughts to every part of your body.

   As you do, invite your spirit guides into your sacred space so that you may come to know them.

Smoke and Fire Readings (cont.)

3. **Light a candle to help reveal the spirits around you.**

    With the candle firmly anchored in the sand, light it.

    See the lighting of the candle as a creative act. You are
    creating light where there was none to help reveal the
    spirits around you.

4. **Holding the charged paper over the candle flame,
    move it around to form patterns of smoke on the
    paper's surface.**

    Until you get the hang of it, you might want to hold
    the paper with tweezers or a pair of those wooden
    toast or muffin retrievers. This will help keep your
    fingers away from the paper if it catches fire.

    Take the parchment in the tongs, holding it by the
    edge. You will be positioning the flat side of the paper
    over the candle (not the paper's edge).

    Slowly lower the paper toward the flame of the candle
    to about an inch or two above it. The flame should be
    close enough that the heat and smoke from the candle
    will accumulate on the paper, but not so close that
    you actually burn the paper.

    This takes practice because it is so easy for the paper
    to catch fire. If the paper starts to burn, pull it away
    from the flame immediately and drop it into the
    bucket of water. If this happens, you will have to
    charge another piece of paper and start over.

Magical Practice

5. **Slowly move the paper around in different patterns and circles over the flame.**

   If you are close enough to the flame, you will be able to see the dark smoke gathering on the other side of the paper.

   Try and cover as much of the middle section of the paper with smoke as possible. It's O.K. to pull the paper away from the flame occasionally and look to see how much coverage there is. You want the smoke coverage to be rather dark.

6. **Now pull the parchment away from the candle flame and turn it over.**

   Be careful not to touch the smoke part, as it will come off on your hands and clothes. If a good portion is covered with smoke, extinguish the flame, unless others are going to try this as well.

7. **Take a comfortable seat and let your eyes gaze at the smoke patterns on the paper.**

   Turn the paper in different ways to see what images appear.

   What do you see?

   Can you see any faces?

   Are there any animals?

   Do any of the patterns resemble anything?

Smoke and Fire Readings (cont.)

Don't worry that it's your imagination. Your Inner Guardian will help you see the images and symbols of your guides that are around you. This is very much like doing the cloud readings, only you are working with smoke. You will see what is important to you.

Take your time with this. You will see images appearing upon the paper. Faces may be spirit guides or people you have known. Trust your instincts. All that appears will relate to your spirit guides in some way because that is what you charged the paper to do.

8. **When you are finished, give thanks to the spirits for showing themselves and close your sacred space.**

This same practice can be done to get insight into other problems. Instead of focusing on spirit guides while you are charging the paper, focus on a particular problem. Ask for guidance to be revealed through the smoke.

Some people like to write questions on the paper themselves and then perform the exercise to see what answer is revealed. When I do demonstrations of this technique, I usually have the people write a question on the back of the paper with their name and birth date. Then I do the work with the fire.

On one occasion, I took a person's parchment and when I looked at the patterns in it, there was a tiny baby,

Smoke and Fire Readings (cont.)

the image of a fetus in the womb. It was very clear. I held it up for the group to see because it was so obvious.

When I turned it over to look at the name and the question. There was a set of initials but no question. When I asked the audience if the person would mind revealing himself or herself, a young woman stood up in the back.

She proceeded to tell the story of how she and her husband had been trying to have a baby for two years. Her question that she charged the paper with was, "Will we have a baby soon?"

From the image on the paper, I told her it was a definite, "yes!" In fact, I told her she was probably pregnant at that time. Three weeks later she confirmed that she was indeed pregnant.

This happens all of the time with this practice!

It is not important
WHO
your guide is, but
WHAT
information
comes through.

Loving Closure

skills developed
- promotes contact with loved ones who have passed on
- helps emotional healing
- brings the past to closure

One of the greatest benefits of working with spirit is the opportunity it provides to bring closure to the past. So often loved ones pass away and we do not get the chance to say good-bye or tell them exactly how we feel. This makes healing difficult.

This exercise is deceptively simple, but very powerful. In it we invite a loved one to come back and speak with us about all of things we did not get a chance to say. Some families do this exercise together and when they compare notes afterward, they are amazed and filled with relief and joy.

- Set the mood.

- Perform a relaxation technique.

1. Create your sacred space.

    Invite the angels to guard and protect you.

2. **Close your eyes and enter the Inner Castle.**

   On the castle grounds is a special place you associate with the loved one who has passed on. Remember that everything is possible in your inner castle.

   When I did this after my father passed away, I went on my castle grounds to a place that was like the home I grew up in. As I went through the house and out the back, my Dad was sitting on the back patio drinking a beer.

3. **Imagine what you would do if you could see this person again.**

   Imagine hugging the person, telling the person what you want to say. Let your imagination run.

   If there are old issues, talk about them. Ask for messages you can give to other members of the family. Ask how you can recognize when this person is nearby

4. **Say goodbye and thank this person.**

5. **Leave this place and return to your sacred space, letting your heart be open and light.**

   Know that the past is healed and that you are no further from this person than you allow.

• **Perform a grounding ritual.**

Record all of your impressions and experiences in your Book of Enchantment.

That place in your
heart where you
tuck away all of
your hopes, wishes,
and dreams is the
most sacred place
you will ever find.

Suggestions for Parents

➤ **Visit a spiritualist church or organization with your young person.**

Spiritualism is still popular in many parts of the world and in the U.S. There are many spiritualist churches and organizations.

As part of their worship service they have a segment known as "Messages from Spirit." Skilled mediums bring forth messages from the spirit world to those in the congregation. Most are safe and nurturing environments to explore and learn about the world of spirit.

➤ **If you have recently lost a loved one, perform the "Loving Closure" magical practice with your family.**

This exercise provides a wonderful opportunity for healing. Create a special gathering with prayers and blessings to send that loving spirit on.

➤ **Do some "Smoke and Fire" readings together.**

This can be great fun and provides terrific conversation. You will also be surprised at what you will uncover and the faces that will appear.

Lesson 6

The Power of Telepathy

What if you could read someone's mind?

How would that change your life?

Can you imagine sending your friends mental messages rather than passing notes?

Telepathy is the ability to send and receive messages and information through the mind. It is mind-to-mind communication. Sometimes these messages are just thoughts, sometimes emotions, and sometimes physical sensations.

Telepathy can be spontaneous, particularly with those we are close to. If you and someone else have thought the same thing at the same time, you have experienced spontaneous telepathy. If you have known who was phoning before answering, again, you have experienced spontaneous telepathy. If you have ever felt a friend's ache or pain when they were not around, once again, you have experienced spontaneous telepathy.

Although most of us have experienced spontaneous telepathy some time in our lives, it can be learned and the communication deliberate. As you work to develop this skill, you will find that although all of you can learn to send and receive, some of you will be better senders and some will be better receivers.

THREE FORMS OF TELEPATHIC COMMUNICATION

MENTAL

sending or experiencing thoughts

EMOTIONAL

sending or experiencing sympathetic feelings

PHYSICAL

sending or experiencing physical sensations

Strengthening Telepathic Connections

Telepathy, in whatever form it takes, works best if the emotions are involved. We often hear stories of parents who experience a psychic link with their children. If something happens to the child, they just "know" it. This is a form of emotional or sympathetic telepathy. Lovers often experience this same thing. If you are developing your telepathic abilities with someone you share strong emotions with, you will experience more success in the beginning. The emotions give a power boost to thoughts.

Don't fret, though, if you do not have a close friend or family member to practice and develop this psychic power with. You can develop your telepathic skills with your pets and even send and receive messages from yourself.

My wife and I have always been able to send and receive mental messages from each other. Sometimes we miss, but at other times we are very good. I think I am a little bit better sender than receiver, but this is probably because I have always had a tendency to be sensitive and so I work to block out most things sent my way. My wife, on the other hand, is an excellent receiver.

When I took my open water, scuba diving test, it was in mid-March at a lake in Ohio. The water temperature was about 45 degrees and the air temperature was not much higher. There was no doubt that my wet suit would not keep me warm at all. She had done her open water diving test in the cold, so before I left for my test, she and I discussed how best to handle the cold. She offered to try and send some warmth my way. I decided since she was open to sending me warmth, I might as well try and send some of my coldness her way as well.

Needless to say, it was cold. I passed my scuba tests, but throughout the morning I was not nearly as cold as I had anticipated. All the others at the test site sure complained about it. I was just thrilled it had gone so well.

When I got back home, I burst through the door, loudly calling out how well I had done. When I stepped into the living room, I found my wife on the couch

Psych Out

THE TELEPATHY
GAME

What is this
man thinking?

bundled up in three blankets. She was shivering and her lips were blue. She had been freezing throughout the morning and had only begun to warm up about the time my test had ended.

We had expected some good results, but I don't think either of us had anticipated just how effectively this would work. To this day, she denies she was trying to be the receiver, but I am sure that's just because that part of her brain probably got too cold. I don't believe she has ever quite forgiven me for that experience. ☺

Checking Your Psychic Links to Others

We often develop psychic links with people we are close to. Emotional closeness opens psychic channels. WE OFTEN SENSE AND FEEL THINGS MORE EASILY WITH THOSE WHO ARE CLOSER TO US. The checklist in the table on the next page will help you to determine if you have a psychic link with a friend, a member of the family, or even a romantic love.

Take a moment or two and focus your attention on a particular person. If you wish, you may both work down the checklists together, focusing on each other. After answering the questions, take time to discuss them. It will strengthen your link.

A *yes* answer to any two of these questions will indicate you enjoy a psychic link with the other person. In time, that link will grow even stronger if you work on it.

Psychic Links

➤ Do you frequently know what the other person is thinking and feeling at times without any verbal communication?

➤ Do you seem to instinctively know when good or bad news is coming the other person's way?

➤ Have you ever experienced sympathetic minor aches or pains at the same time the other person was experiencing discomfort?

➤ When separated from the other person, are you sometimes able to know if he or she is having difficulty and wants to call you?

➤ Do you seem to know what the other person has done during the day while you were away without any prior knowledge or hints?

➤ Does the other person sometimes act on your unspoken desires or wishes within a short while after you have focused upon them yourself?

➤ Do you and the other person frequently say the same things at the same time?

➤ Have you ever sensed when the other person was hiding feelings or thoughts and later discovered you were correct?

➤ Do you find it difficult to truly surprise the other person?

➤ Can you tell when the other person is talking or thinking about you?

A *yes* to six or more of the questions indicates an exceptional psychic link between the two of you. Don't try and hide things from each other; you likely will not succeed. ☺ **The stronger the relationship, the stronger the telepathic connection!**

Using Telepathy with Your Pets

You don't need to confine your telepathic communication to your human friends. Animals have highly developed sensitivities, easily picking up on subtleties around them. They are gifted with heightened senses as part of their survival instinct. Homing pigeons always find their way back home. When out in a field, horses sense electrical changes through their feet and are able to avoid lightning strikes. Dogs and cats can tell whether humans fear them.

I work with birds of prey and hold state and federal permits to keep and use hawks and owls in educational programs. Because they will be with me in public situations, they have to be socialized—trained to be around humans. They are not pets and so being around humans is not natural for them. They have to develop trust.

In the past, one of the ways I have trained hawks and owls to trust and be around humans is by bringing them indoors while I go about my daily activities. This gets them used to human movement and activity so they are less likely to be nervous in front of groups. I am always amazed at how sensitive they are. I have found that the wilder the animals are, the more instinctually and psychically sensitive they are. My hawks are always first in picking up the presence of spirit in my home. Their heads will turn in unison in the direction of spirit.

*Spending time to play and work with your pets
helps build a psychic link with them.
This link then becomes the foundation for
developing your own telepathic abilities.*

My cats are the next most sensitive to spirit. Cats have been domesticated for a far shorter period of time than dogs, so are still fairly quick at sensing the presence of spirit. My dogs, on the other hand, are kind of "doh-dee-doh-dee-doh." They are just a bit slow in picking it up—bless their hearts.

Because all animals (well, except perhaps for my dogs) sense subtle changes in the environment around them, they are extremely sensitive to emotions. This makes pets great assistants in developing your own telepathic abilities. In fact, working with animals is one of the easiest ways to develop your skill. Remember, though, the key is the stronger the relationship, the stronger the telepathic connection.

You can build a solid foundation for telepathic links with your pets or other domesticated animals by spending time with them and by refraining from forcing the connection. Wild animals, as discussed above, require different techniques and are much more difficult to work with. If you develop telepathy with your pet, though, it will be easier to do so later with wild animals.

SPEND TIME WITH YOUR ANIMALS

I can't say this often enough. The stronger the relationship you have with an animal (or a person), the stronger your telepathic connection will be.

I have always been good with animals. I am typical of those who are said to "have a way with animals." I'm not sure exactly why this is, but I realized years ago when I began doing regular obedience training with my dogs the telepathic communication strengthened tremendously. The time spent learning with the dog was one key to the communication that developed. The dog learned about my voice and touch and came to understand the subtleties of my gestures and postures. It learned how I thought. I came to know the dog as well.

Every dog is different and responds uniquely to obedience commands. Some require a firm approach, some a more playful one. My efforts to train the dogs developed a rapport with them. I was able to understand their personalities and essences more fully and likewise, they mine. This made it easier to use telepathy with them.

Cats are much more independent than dogs and early playtime and regular touching of the animals when they are young establishes the telepathic connection. It is very difficult to develop telepathy with a cat that has not been touched or petted much, especially as a kitten.

When working with animals, playtime is essential. Without it, you do your animals an injustice and are not going to be able to establish much of a telepathic link. Even the training should be treated as fun. Everything is easier if we enjoy doing it. Playtime is as essential for animals as for humans. Without it animals—and we as well—become crotchety and self-centered. This blocks psychic perceptions.

Never Force Connections

Let the animal set the tone and rhythm of the time spent together. With animals, the connection must be established before the telepathy can truly begin, especially when it comes to trust. However, connections should never be forced.

A number of years ago I was doing a workshop on my book *Animal-Speak* at a center in Florida. One of the participants brought a dog that had been ill, hoping I would do some healing work on it. People at the workshop got up and started rushing over to the dog, oohing and ahhing. I felt a lot the people were putting on a show to demonstrate to me they were true animal people. The dog tried to get away and finally hid in the back. I didn't do anything. I didn't even approach the dog. As the workshop went on, the dog began to edge closer. By the end of the seminar, the dog was laying next to my bag underneath the front table.

I cannot count how many times I have been told not to get upset if a particular animal doesn't take to me. Inevitably the animals does come to me. If you send comforting thoughts of safety toward animals, they will respond accordingly. Let the animal approach you. It needs to feel comfortable. Telepathy works best if there is a genuine trust and feeling of safety between the partners, whether it's an animal or a person.

Psychic Science

CRYSTALS

Crystals are an important part of the modern electronic age. Crystal chips are essential to radio, television, radar, watches, computers and most electronic devices associated with communication in some form or another. Crystals have the ability to handle energy with great precision.

What if we had something like a crystal to amplify our thoughts?

What if we had a simple device to help us send and receive messages as thoughts?

Marcel Vogel, a former senior scientist with IBM, researched liquid crystals and the nature of thought. He concluded that crystals harmonize and align our thoughts and energies.

Quartz crystals have within them a natural ability to focus and amplify most types of energies. The human body is regulated by the pulse and flow of energy, so it is only natural to try and influence body energies with crystals.

So what does this mean for us?

It means that you can use crystals to amplify your send and receive energies. Take a simple quartz crystal point. While relaxed, holding it in both hands with the point upward, visualize it amplifying and projecting your thoughts outward.

To receive, we should sit in a relaxed position and hold the crystal in both hands with the point downward. Pay attention to your thoughts and feelings as you become a receiving station.

ergo:

QUARTZ CRYSTALS
CAN BE USED TO DEVELOP
TELEPATHY!

*Magical
Practice*

Chakra Hook-Up

**skills
developed**

- strengthens psychic links
- enables easier telepathy
- helps build a more intimate connection

Sooner or later you are going to come across this strange word *chakra*. It is an Eastern Sanskrit word that means *wheel*. One of the easiest ways to understand the chakras is to think of them as individual radar terminals for the computer we call our mind.

There are seven major chakras in our body, each controlling different body systems and levels of the subconscious mind. They are centers of energy activity in the body, handling all life energies for us. All energies experienced outside of the body are picked up by one of these chakra centers and linked to the mind. There the information is gathered and stored in our subconscious. We can access that information through development of our psychic powers.

When we align our chakras with another person's, we are also attuning all of our basic body energies and systems with the other person's, making us more compat-

CHAKRA CENTERS OF THE BODY

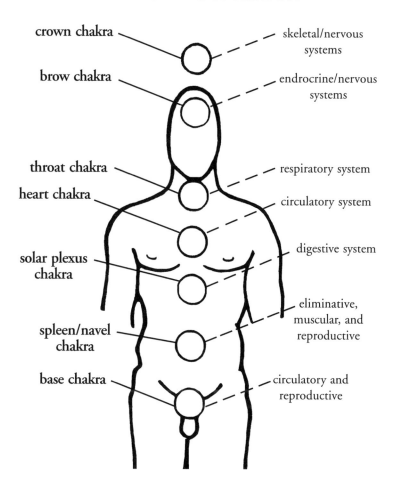

crown chakra — skeletal/nervous systems

brow chakra — endrocrine/nervous systems

throat chakra — respiratory system

heart chakra — circulatory system

solar plexus chakra — digestive system

spleen/navel chakra — eliminative, muscular, and reproductive

base chakra — circulatory and reproductive

The chakras mediate all energies within the body and assimilate all of the energies outside of the body. Each is a little radar system that feeds the big computer of the mind. They operate in front and behind us in their location of the body.

223

Magical Practice

ible to each other. It becomes easier then to send and receive messages. It's similar to putting all your computer files in the same format as a friend's so you can both read them.

When we align the chakras, we are strengthening our connection to the other person. We become more compatible—more in tune with each other. This happens naturally with time between most friends and couples, but the hook-up is even stronger when we perform this exercise regularly.

For this exercise you will need a partner, someone to practice with. You will also need two chairs so you can each be seated from one to three feet apart and facing each other.

ALIGNING THE CHAKRAS

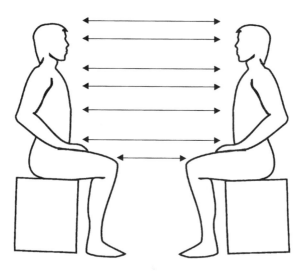

Chakra Hook-Up (cont.)

SHARING ENERGIES:
BUILDING CONNECTIONS

• **Together create a sacred space.**

Protect the space with the calling to the angels or with some other prayer or affirmation.

• **Slowly begin a progressive relaxation.**

Watch the other person's breathing and try to match your own to it. Some find it beneficial to inhale as the other exhales and vice versa. Don't be afraid to experiment.

1. **Beginning with the crown chakra at the top of your head, visualize it being linked to the other person's.**

I use a stream of light. Others use silk threads. Visualize it in any way you wish, but both of you should agree on this before you start.

Feel your chakras connecting. Imagine it in your mind. Know that as you do, you are linking more strongly to the other person. As you make the crown chakra connection, speak the name of the person you are connecting to in a soft voice.

2. Next, visualize moving down to the area of the brow
    chakra and make a connection, speaking the name of
    the person softly.

    Continue making the rest of the chakra connections
    in the same manner, slowly moving down the body:
    the throat, the heart, the solar plexus, the navel, the
    base of the spine or groin.

3. Now, just feel yourself connected to the other
    person.

    Look into the other person's eyes. Feel yourself at one
    with him or her.

4. Keep this connection for about 2 to 3 minutes (this
    whole process should take no more than 12 to 15
    minutes).

    With practice you will become faster. You will find
    that some people are easier to connect with than
    others are. This is natural.

    Pay attention to any feelings or thoughts that come to
    mind throughout the connecting process. Make note
    of them, but try and stay focused on the connections.

Chakra Hook-Up (cont.)

5. **Now begin the disconnecting, starting at the base of your spine, drawing your energy of light back into you.**

    Feel yourself disconnecting from the other person. Then moving upward, disconnect the navel, then the solar plexus, heart, throat, brow and crown.

*   **Perform a grounding ritual by stretching, relaxing, and discussing what you each felt or experienced.**

    Make mention of any emotions or thoughts that came to mind in the process. You both might even want to hug at this point.

Do not practice this more than once or twice at a session. When you get good at this, try the hookup while in separate rooms.

Magical Practice

Partnering

skills developed

- develops ability to send and receive
- strengthens relationships
- boosts psychic abilities

Emotional or sympathetic telepathy is one of the easiest skills to develop. It is usually already in place between parent and child and between trusted friends and lovers.

We learned how to connect chakras to enhance sympathetic telepathy in the "Chakra Hook-Up" exercise. Here you will actually start practicing receiving information with these connections in mind, and in the variations, actually sending information.

Partnering to Develop
Telepathic Abilities

- Create a sacred space.

- Perform a relaxation and meditation together.

1. Perform the chakra hook-up.

2. One of you closes your eyes and focuses on some recent emotional incident.

   This could perhaps be a quarrel, a pleasant surprise, or a frightening encounter. Just be careful not to give any clues about the incident.

   Concentrate on this incident for three to four minutes. Feel the emotions of the incident you have in mind as strongly as possible. Do not try and send the feelings to the other person, but just feel them within yourself.

3. Open your eyes and have your partner describe what he or she thinks your mood or emotion was.

4. Repeat this same procedure three to four times and then switch roles.

- Perform a grounding ritual.

Magical Practice

VARIATION: TARGET PRACTICE

There are several fun variations on "Partnering." In "Partnering," you were not actually trying to send your feelings to your partner, but seeing if your partner could pick up on what you were feeling. In this variation, which I call "Target Practice," you will actually be sending the information to your partner.

- **Prepare for this exercise just as you did in "Partnering."**

- **After preparing, decide who will be sender and who will be receiver to start.**

  You will by trading places so each has a chance to do the sending.

1. **Select a part of your partner's body as a target, close your eyes, and focus intensely upon it.**

   Imagine tickling or lightly pinching that part of your partner's body. Spend about two to three minutes on three to four different parts of your partner's body.

   Sometimes it helps to first imagine yourself experiencing the tickling or pinching sensation in that part of your own body. Concentrate on feeling it yourself before projecting it to your partner.

Partnering (cont.)

2. **When you are finished sending information, open your eyes and compare notes about what your partner felt.**

3. **Switch roles and let your partner target parts of your body.**

• **Perform a grounding ritual.**

   Close your sacred space, stretch, and relax a bit.

Take the time to record your results in your Book of Enchantment.

Concentrate on having fun while practicing. Do not make this into a contest because doing so will affect your ability to send and receive.

If you get good at "Target Practice," try projecting and receiving simple geometric shapes (circle, square, triangle, star) for three to four minutes at a time to each other. Visualize drawing them on paper, on the person, or in some form such as that. Some people find that if they sit with a pencil and paper while receiving, they will end up doodling the correct form. Also try this exercise while in separate rooms.

Magical Practice

Sending Yourself a Message

skills developed
- strengthens your ability to be a telepathic receiver
- helps develop an inner telepathic warning system

This is a wonderful little exercise to send messages to your Inner Guardian. It can become your personal reminder for important events and serve as an inner warning or alert system.

- **When you go to bed at night, create in   your mind a sacred space around you.**

    This is generally a good practice to do anyway. It will help you sleep more deeply and peacefully.

    You may also find it helpful to call upon the angels for a peaceful night's sleep and to assist you throughout the night.

1. **Visualize yourself connecting to your Inner Guardian.**

   Some people mentally do a chakra hook-up with their Guardian, but this isn't necessary—it's all a part of you.

2. **Decide on the time you wish to wake up in the morning and visualize yourself waking up at that time, rested and alert.**

3. **Then just go to sleep.**

   The first few times you will still want to set the alarm clock or only do this when you do not have to be anywhere first thing in the morning.

   If you wake up during the night, just take a look at the clock. Sometimes with this practice your Inner Guardian becomes a little overanxious. After several times, though, you will start to find yourself waking within a half hour of the scheduled time.

When I travel, I usually have a very hectic schedule teaching in a different city each day, so I can't miss getting on the road by a particular time. I use this method along with the hotel alarm clock and wake-up call system. I send a message to wake myself up a half-hour before I have to. I set the alarm for a half-hour past that and I also ask for a wake-up call from the hotel desk. The telepathic message is my primary wake-up. The alarm clock and the phone call then become snooze alarms for me just in case I need a few more minutes of sleep. It works very well.

*Magical
Practice*

Long Distance Healing

**skills
developed**
- enhances thought and energy projection
- develops responsibility

Healing is something everyone who involves themselves in the psychic or magical life should learn to do. It balances us and helps keep us from becoming too self-centered. It is also one of the best ways to develop intuition.

Long distance healing truly enhances telepathic ability. People are often asked to send prayers and healing energies to those not present. Although this seems an unreal possibility to some people, it is really very effective. Long distance healing is a wonderful way to develop your focus when telepathically sending energy to others.

Be aware, though, that you should **never** send thoughts, emotions, healings, or prayers to anyone without their permission. No one has the right to intrude into the lives of others. Intruding into other people's lives without their specific permission, even with healing messages, is no different from getting unwanted phone calls. Remember how you felt the last time someone kept calling you and pestering you to do something you had already said no to.

No one has the right to project energies to us without our permission. Occasionally there are those who do try. As long as you keep yourself balanced, you will not have a problem. Go into your sacred space, call upon the angels, and ask your Inner Guardian to block it all out. You will see the situation change.

If you are asked to send energy and are unsure if you should even though you've been asked to, attach a qualifier: "I ask that this energy be used for the good of all according to the free will of all." In this way, the recipient of your projections is not being intruded upon.

Magical Practice

SENDING OTHERS
GOOD ENERGY

• **Make your preparations and create your sacred space.**

Call upon the angels for your protection and the well being of the person to whom you are going to project energies. Ask that this healing be done for the good of all, according to the free will of all.

• **Perform a progressive relaxation.**

See and feel yourself warm, relaxed, strong and healthy.

1. **Bring the person to mind, visualizing this person before you, and begin to do a chakra hook-up with this individual.**

Start with the crown and move downward and remember to speak the person's name with each connection.

2. **Once you are hooked up, begin slow rhythmic breathing.**

Inhale for a count of four, hold for a count of four, and exhale for a count of four.

Long Distance Healing (cont.)

As you inhale, see and feel crystalline healing light from the divine streaming down into you to heal, strengthen, and bless you.

As you exhale, that wonderful healing energy streams forth from you through each of the chakra connections into the other person to balance, heal, strengthen. and bless that person.

Continue this for about five minutes. See and feel that person strong and vibrant, healed of the problem.

3. **Offer a prayer of thanks for the healing and begin disconnecting, pulling your energy back.**

• **Bring your focus back to you and your sacred space.**

Take a moment to see and feel yourself healed and strengthened by this process.

As you work with this exercise, you may feel like doing parts a bit differently. Find a variation that works best for you.

Magical Practice

Pet Telepathy

skills developed
- develops telepathy
- lays the foundation for improved animal communication

In the past five to six years, more and more *animal communicators* have appeared on the scene, those who either telepathically communicate with the spirit of an animal or perform psychic readings by tuning into a person's pet. This exercise can be used to lay the foundation for becoming an animal communicator and can also be adapted to locate and call missing pets back to us if it's possible for them to return.

Do not be afraid to experiment. When performed outdoors, this exercise can be used to call your spirit animal or totem to you.

GETTING CLOSE
TO YOUR PET

- **Make your preparations.**

  Make sure that you are in a different room from your dog or cat.

- **Create your sacred space.**

  Call the angels into the environment.

- **Begin your progressive relaxation.**

1. **Begin the chakra hook-up.**

   There is a difference in connecting the chakras with people and connecting with an animal. We will use four connections.

   Start by visualizing your crown chakra connecting with the crown chakra of your pet. As you make each connection, whisper or speak softly the name of your pet.

2. **Then connect your solar plexus to a point about halfway down the spine or underside of the animal.**

   The solar plexus center in humans is linked to our emotions, and animals respond strongly to emotions, so this is the most powerful center for linking with animals.

3. **Continue the hook-up by linking the base of your spine with the base of your pet's spine.**

4. **Link the chakras in the arches of your feet with the feet of your pet.**

   The hook-up is a bit different. The seven chakras we worked with before are the major ones, but we have others, including the small chakras in the arches of our feet.

5. **Once you have made the four chakra connections, visualize your pet coming to visit you.**

   Feel your pet excited to see you and you excited to see it. Imagine it coming into your sacred space where you are sitting. Call it to you in your mind.

   Continue this visualization for about five minutes or until your pet arrives. When it does, make sure you reward it with wonderful petting and loving. Thank it for coming to you, for responding to your thoughts.

   Do not be discouraged if your pet doesn't happen to arrive at first.

Pet Telepathy (cont.)

6. **Disconnect slowly from your pet's chakras, reversing the direction you hooked up, moving from your feet, back up to your base, your solar plexus, and your crown.**

    Call your energy back to you.

    Thank the angels for helping, if only to assist in making your pet more receptive.

*   **Perform a grounding ritual.**

If your pet did not come to you, go and find it. Take note of what it is doing. Has it moved at all since you started the exercise? Is it closer to you?

Take some time here and give your pet some loving attention. Sometimes the process is confusing to the animal, and it is not sure what to do. Your petting helps to let it know that it is O.K. to visit you when it hears the call.

Telepathic Shopping

On the day I was finishing up this chapter, my wife had gone into town to do the grocery shopping. It had been a hectic week and with all of the activities, I had forgotten to tell her to buy some Kleenex. Summer allergies were active. I had just cut the back fields, and earlier this week I had stacked 200 bales of hay in my barn. Needless to say, I was sneezing and blowing my nose a lot.

Rather than go back to the store again later, I thought that it would be good to try and send her the message through telepathy. I figured what better day to do it than when I am writing a chapter on the subject.

I calmed myself and performed a chakra hook-up. Then I spoke her name softly. I visualized her taking boxes of tissue off the shelf and placing them in her grocery cart. I visualized myself sneezing and blowing my nose and the box of tissues being paid for and brought home.

Several hours later, when I helped her unload the car, I discovered she had bought three boxes. I started laughing and told her what I had done. She said that when she walked down the aisle, all she kept seeing was me blowing my nose.

The telepathy worked!

Unfortunately though, she forgot to buy the toilet paper.

Suggestions for Parents

➤ **Send messages to your young person to call.**

Softly repeat their name as you visualize them dialing the phone for you.

➤ **When your young person is at the grocery store, visualize them picking up and putting an item in their basket.**

Quietly repeat their name as you do this.

➤ **Perform the "Partnering" exercise with the young person in your life.**

➤ **Go to a metaphysical store with your young person and purchase some quartz crystals.**

Use the crystals to amplify your thoughts and feelings as you do the "Partnering"exercise together.

Lesson 7

Precautions and Protections

Do I need to worry about seeing bad things and not being able to do anything about it?

What if I have visions that I don't understand?

What happens if I'm afraid of what I perceive?

What if others do not understand me?

Will psychic ability make me over-emotional?

How do I determine my own feelings from others?

Psychic power can be a wonderful thing, giving you glimpses of all the possibilities and opportunities for choice in your life and alerting you to things which may not be what they seem. But please don't think that psychic power, in and of itself, is going to make your life a piece of cake by solving all your problems. You are always the one in control of your psychic life and the one responsible for making the choices. Nonetheless, creating the magical life allows you to see that there are realms more wonderful than most of us can imagine.

The only real valuable thing is intuition

Albert Einstein

A great deal of mystery still surrounds the magical and psychic world. In your exploration of these things, you may become the brunt of jokes by people who do not understand and are more than likely afraid of the unknown or of change. However, with the development of your psychic abilities, the potential to awaken tremendous creative and magical power is always within your reach. Development of your psychic power can help you bring many wonderful benefits into your life:

➢ improved health,

➢ decreased stress,

➢ more informed decisions,

➢ better control of life's events,

➢ increased creativity,

➢ awakened creative potentials,

➢ energized relaxation,

➢ broader perspective on life,

➢ access to past life information,

➢ enhanced spiritual development,

➢ increased balance,

➢ greater control of life's energies,

➢ increased discernment and discrimination,

➢ opportunities to assist others, and

➢ recognition of higher forces within life.

YOUR MAGICAL SELVES

I am the Hero of my life.
I am always more creative and capable
than I imagine.

Hero

I am the Warrior of my life.
I respond to all things with courage,
responsibility, and endurance.

Warrior

Wise One

I am the Wise One in my life.
I bring great understanding and
confidence to all I do.

Magician

I am the Magician of my life.
I perceive everything around me with
balance and insight

Handling Psychic Power

As many benefits as there are to developing psychic power, most people will still have three issues to deal with when they begin to work with their natural abilities. Young and old, we have to learn how to handle our sensitivities, face our fears, and honor our self worth.

As you awaken your psychic power, you will need to pay particular attention to these areas. Unlike most people, though, you will have the four aspects of your magical self discussed in Volume I, *Magic of Believing*, to help you address these issues. If you remember, these four aspects are The Hero, The Warrior, The Magician, and The Wise One.

By exploring the psychic realm, you are becoming The Hero. When it comes to developing your psychic power, The Hero part of you will be able to call upon The Magician, Warrior and Wise One when needed. To keep The Hero in you strong, say these affirmations here three times.

I am The Hero in my life
I am always more creative and capable than I imagine.

THE MAGICIAN HELPS CONTROL
YOUR PSYCHIC SENSITIVITY

Understanding what you perceive accurately is a large part of psychic development. Another part is learning to control it so you can turn it on and off at will and don't become too psychically sensitive or drained. You may call upon The Magician within to help you.

Psychic development will also increase your potential for empathic responses to people and places around you. Things you used to be able to ignore you may no longer be able to. You may see and feel things you do not want to know about. You may discover things you might wish you had never learned. But the benefits far outweigh the disadvantages if you are willing to deal with these issues as they arise.

The Magician will help you to see, know, and experience many new wonders and possibilities. Working with psychic power will make you more sensitive to everything going on around you.

As your psychic abilities grow stronger, The Magician part of you will grow stronger too. If you find yourself becoming too sensitive, visualize yourself as The Magician, calling upon that part of yourself and say the affirmations here three times.

I am The Magician of my life.
I perceive everything around me with balance and insight.

THE WARRIOR HELPS YOU
FACE YOUR FEARS

Fear is a part of life, part of our survival instinct, making us alert and perceptive. Fear only becomes a negative when we allow it to go beyond watching and alerting us to possibilities and let it control our life and behavior. It becomes a problem when we allow it to get out of hand. The only way to dispel fear is to bring it out in the open and face it. Once you recognize the fear, you can often let it go. As you begin to explore the psychic realm, you will likely have to face some of your fears, possibly some you have kept hidden even from yourself.

You may experience things you have never seen or felt before. Questions and doubts about what you are learning may creep into your mind. When this happens, call upon The Warrior inside of you. Warriors are strong and responsible. They take it upon themselves to get things done no matter what the difficulties. They persist. They find ways to make things work. They don't give up just because something is difficult—only if it is foolish.

While you are developing your psychic powers, you will see both the good and the bad. And like The Warrior, you will need to take on the responsibility of dealing with both. If you find yourself unsure what to do, visualize yourself as The Warrior and say the affirmations here three times.

I am The Warrior of my life.
I respond to all things with courage,
responsibility, and endurance.

THE WISE ONE HELPS YOU RECOGNIZE YOUR SELF-WORTH

If you haven't yet experienced feeling different from others, as you develop your psychic abilities, there will

come a time when you will. Just remember you are not really different—we all have psychic sensitivities. The only difference is that you have chosen to explore your psychic potentials. You are most likely feeling different because you have chosen to pursue abilities most people don't bother with.

Even though you really aren't any different from other people, we live in a society which just doesn't tolerate variation well. Any deviation from what is considered ordinary behavior may result in ridicule. This can cause us to feel lost or out of place and even destroy our confidence in ourselves. We can grow to feel less than what we really are.

On the other hand, if our ego tries to help us feel special to cover up our lack of self-confidence, there will be problems. Earlier in this book we talked about the psychics who tried to portray their power as something special, a cosmic gift no one else has. This outlook is often described as being *out of balance*. The ego is a powerful thing. Statements about being special all reflect a person's ego trying to paper over a low sense of self-worth. This is the ego's attempt to make that "out of place" feeling become one of "acceptable uniqueness."

If you are feeling out of place or unbalanced as you develop your psychic powers, draw upon the wisdom of The Wise One within you. The Wise One already knows you are wonderfully creative. Developing your natural psychic abilities simply helps you tap into those tremendously creative parts of yourself in ways beyond what is recognized or accepted by society.

There will always be things in our lives we cannot control, that we have to adjust to. The Wise One can help us choose the best of the possibilities and opportunities in these kinds of situations. Developing our psychic powers enables us to more easily tune in to this guidance, gaining a knowledge and understanding of our inner power which will be the key to our success throughout our life.

Call upon The Wise One within you when you need to believe more in yourself or overcome other people's misperceptions of you. Visualize yourself as The Wise One and say the affirmations here three times.

I am The Wise One of my life.

I bring great understanding and confidence to all I do.

When Psychic Sensitivity Becomes Empathic

We all experience times of empathy in our life, but most of us usually don't recognize them or understand them when they occur. Some people are empathic all of their life, and not understanding what is occurring, they assume something is wrong with them.

If you are sitting next to someone who has a headache and you are empathic, you begin to feel that person's headache. This feeling is so strong you actually get a headache. You mistake the other person's headache for your own. You may not even realize the headache you have was psychically picked up from the person beside you!

With empathy, someone else's physical feelings, emotions, and attitudes can register so strongly upon us that we assume these are our own feelings. We often don't realize that what we are feeling may actually be tied to someone we encountered or the location we are in, or any number of other possibilities. What we are feeling is not an actual headache, but a psychic impression of someone else's headache.

Life conditions, physiological changes, and psychic development heighten our natural sensitivities. When we become more empathic, the aura grows more magnetic so outside impressions register upon us much more strongly and intensely than they normally would. For those involved in psychic development and healing

Imagine if...

- You could live a life of magic,

- You were experiencing life to the fullness of your potentials,

- You were living the power in your name, your life, your essence, and your possibilities!

work, it is important to recognize this natural tendency to be empathic. It is very easy to link with the problems and issues of others and then to carry them with us as if they are our own. If we are not aware of this tendency, we can begin to think we are going crazy (and so do other people because of our mood swings).

If you find that there is a strong tendency to be empathic, there are several things you can do.

Deliberately Disconnect from Others Every Day

At the end of the day, create your sacred space and visualize yourself in some way disconnecting from everyone with whom you have had an encounter. Some like to visualize this as a cutting of threads or a pulling out cords from the other person. You can even go into your castle and close the gates to everyone.

We should even disconnect from family members and loved ones. We will reconnect again, but if we are empathic, we need to have some time every day in which we are not linked to others at all. This enables us to be more objective and feel a little less crazy.

Use Aromatherapy to Help Soften your Sensitivity

If we are going through empathic times, we should always have two essential oils on hand, gardenia and eucalyptus. Gardenia oil helps us to remain objective while dealing with others. It strengthens the aura and helps prevent us from being drawn into other's prob-

Are You Empathic?

Use the following checklist to get an idea of how empathic you might be. If you answer yes to two or more of the questions, you should consider yourself somewhat empathic and you should take the necessary precautions described in this lesson.

➤ Are you easily persuaded by others doing things you normally wouldn't do, like buy purple sneakers?

➤ Are you overly shy?

➤ Do your moods change as you go from one group of friends to another?

➤ Do you feel drained after being around other people?

➤ Do you always seem to know what others are feeling?

➤ Do animals take to you?

➤ Have you ever felt others watching you even though you didn't see them?

➤ Are you a touchy-feely kind of person?

➤ Can you tell when something of yours is out of place even before you've seen it?

➤ Do you have a hard time telling how you truly feel at any particular time?

➤ Are you overly emotional, taking everything more personally and seriously than others seem to?

➤ Do you have a tendency to take on everyone else's problems, aches, pains, worries, and battles?

lems. Many professional healers, psychics and social workers use gardenia oil for these reasons. Just a tiny drop, diluted in water and worn, is all that is necessary.

Eucalyptus oil makes us less emotional by taking the edge off of what we are experiencing psychically. We still experience the emotions, but in a much more controlled way. Those who are empathic will sleep more easily at night as well. Just put a drop or two in a bowl of water in your bedroom while you sleep

What is psychic
is not always spiritual.

What is occult or metaphysical
is not always uplifting.

What is appealing
is not always beneficial.

Psychic Science

KID POWER

Young people often have accidents in which they lose a fingertip in a slammed car door or an electric fan. Usually, the fingertip is reattached in surgery if it can be found, or the end of the finger is simply stitched close.

In the early 1970s, a child's finger was not sewn back as it normally would have been in English hospital because of a clerical mix-up. Several days passed before the child saw a surgeon.

What do you imagine happened?

Amazingly, the fingertip had begun regenerating—growing back on its own!

By 1974, Dr. Cynthia Illingworth documented several hundred regrown fingertips in children 11 years old and younger. The fingertips grew back perfectly as long as they were not cut off beyond the outermost joint.

Since then, a small number of hospitals are treating these kinds of accidents by allowing the young person's body to use it's own natural power to regenerate the fingertip as good as new.

So what does this show scientists and us?

This shows we all are much more powerful than we often realize. We can heal and do amazing things naturally.

ERGO:

OUR POWER IS ONLY
LIMITED BY OUR BELIEFS!

261

Common Sense Precautions

As with most of life, many problems can be prevented by developing certain qualities and incorporating certain activities within our life. The same is true of psychic development. Most of these recommendations are really just common sense.

➤ **Take care of your physical self.**

Keep the vitality and energy high through proper diet, exercise, fresh air and such.

➤ **Try to develop greater self-confidence in all areas of your life.**

These qualities make us more decisive.

➤ **Whenever you feel uncomfortable, honor that feeling.**

Don't be afraid to examine what you feel and why.

➤ **Educate yourself by asking questions and exploring.**

Don't accept anything blindly. Seek out answers and explanations.

Remember—no one knows what's best for you better than yourself, and no one is doing anything you can't also be doing in your own unique way!

The Blessing Way

The Blessing Way is an ancient phrase for leading a life of creativity and balance, a life dedicated to a purpose that would bless the world in some way.

When we explore our potentials, we break down our old walls and limitations. When we seek out new realms, we discover the creative power of our imagination. When we follow our heart and pursue our dreams, we uncover our sacred self. And the magic within us begins to shine

This is the Blessing Way. This is why we explore our possibilities. This is why we develop our psychic power. It leads us to way of life that blesses us and the world around us.

Know Thyself!

Magical Practice

Psychic Breath

skills developed
- balances
- restores lost energy temporarily
- stimulates psychic ability
- good for memory

In the practice of yoga, breathing is used to balance the male and female energies, the electric and magnetic. When both aspects are balanced, we are healed and strengthened and the state is called *susumna*. Combining a moon breath (magnetic energies, or *ida*) with a sun breath (electric energies, or *pingala*), we quickly energize the aura and balance out our electro-magnetic energies.

Fresh air and proper breathing is essential to the vibrancy and strength of the aura. This yoga breathing technique, sometimes called alternate *nostril breathing*, is wonderfully effective for a quick fix when our energy drops or is suddenly drained.

Nostril breathing energizes our entire system whereas mouth breathing makes us more susceptible to health problems. Air we breathe through our mouth does not pass through the filter of our nose hair and is not warmed by passing through our sinuses.

With this technique, you will be breathing alternately out or each nostril, inhaling through one nostril, holding the breath, and then exhaling out the opposite nostril. The effects of this exercise are greatly enhanced by performing it outdoors in the fresh air. It will improve memory, allowing you to learn material information more quickly and retain it longer, so is an excellent exercise to do before studying.

For this exercise, no preparation is actually necessary. Yes, it is enhanced by creating a sacred space and performing a relaxation, but it's greatest benefit is that it can be performed spontaneously whenever needed.

Magical Practice

1. Begin with a slow exhale and place the tongue at the roof of the mouth behind the front teeth.

    This tongue position helps link our energy pathways, also called *meridians*, which enhances the energizing effects of this breathing technique.

2. Using your thumb, close your right nostril and inhale slowly through your left nostril for a count of four.

    For most people, using the thumb and fingers to close and open the nostrils will be easiest.

3. Keeping the right nostril closed, use your fingers to close down the left nostril so both nostrils are closed for a count of eight.

4. Keeping your left nostril closed, remove your thumb from the right nostril and exhale for a slow count of four.

5. Then switch nostrils with this process, closing down the left nostril and inhaling through the right nostril slowly for a count of four.

Psychic Breath (cont.)

6. Close the right nostril and with both nostrils closed, hold for a count of eight.

7. Keeping the right nostril closed, remove your thumb from the left nostril and exhale slowly for a count of four.

8. Repeat this breathing technique four to five times, alternately inhaling and exhaling through one nostril and then the other.

•   Perform your grounding technique.

When finished, move slowly, for there may be some initial dizziness. If so, it will pass quickly. The energy will build over the following few minutes before it stabilizes. This breathing technique will saturate your aura and your body with quick energy.

Magical Practice

Yin and Yang

skills developed
- balances oversensitivity
- grounds

Yin and Yang, an ancient symbol from the East, are a wonderful meditation tool for balancing psychic energies. Yin, the black side, is a symbol of the feminine or intuitive energies and the earth. Yang, the white side, is a symbol of the masculine and the spirit. Together, Yin and Yang are in balance within the circle, a symbol representing the circular relationship of the physical to spiritual, representing reincarnation, and balance itself.

We are all a combination of physical and spiritual, masculine and feminine energies. If we become oversensitive in our psychic development, this symbol can help us to balance out these energies.

In my castle, I have several chambers and gardens devoted to Eastern traditions. One of my meditative rooms has the Yin and Yang symbol painted over an entire wall.

BALANCING MASCULINE AND FEMININE ENERGIES

- Create your sacred space.

- Perform a progressive relaxation.

1. Visualize the Yin and Yang symbol before you, and as you do, see and feel everything around you being restored to balance.

   Maintain this visual image for about five to eight minutes.

2. After the five to eight minutes, visualize this symbol melting into you in the middle of your chest.

   See and feel yourself balanced and know that whenever you close your eyes and envision the Yin and Yang symbol inside you, it will begin to spin softly to restore balance around you.

3. Give thanks for your restored balance.

- Perform a grounding technique

VARIATION

Focus on the Yin and Yang symbol as you perform the "Psychic Breath" exercise. As you inhale, focus on the dark half (the Yin). As you exhale, focus on the light half (the Yang). This strengthens your psychic breathing and stimulates your psychic perceptions without making you overly sensitive.

Magical Practice

Erasing Problems

skills developed
- solves problems
- eases psychic sensitivities
- strengthens visualization ability

Chalkboards, painter's canvas, computer screens, and television monitors can all be used to help clarify and solve problems. We can learn to visualize these things and send the message to our Inner Guardian to write, paint, type, or show us the answer. One of the easiest and most enjoyable ways to dispel the problems in our lives it to imagine just erasing them away as if we were cleaning off a classroom chalk board.

When I was teaching junior high school, all of the teachers had to have a club that we met with a couple times a month. My club was the ESP club. I taught this exercise to them and they had great success with it.

CLEANING THE
BLACKBOARD

- **Create your sacred space.**

  Call your angels for protection and guidance.

- **Perform a progressive relaxation and close your eyes.**

  You may want to perform your   psychic breath at this point.

1. **Imagine yourself standing before a large chalkboard.**

   Some people imagine a large computer screen or painter's canvas.

2. **Take the chalk and draw out your problem or question, or imagine typing it out on a keyboard.**

   If you use the keyboard image, when you hit the "enter" key after typing your question, think of it as sending the question to your Inner Guardian.

3. **Imagine taking a step back from the chalkboard and taking a seat as you visualize your Inner Guardian stepping into the room, greeting you, and turning to your question.**

   You watch as the answer begins to be written. Trust what you feel here. Even if you can't actually visualize the answer in your mind, trust that the message has been sent (telepathically) to your Inner Guardian. Within a day you should have the answer or guidance you need.

Magical Practice

Erasing Problems (cont.)

4. **Thank your Inner Guardian and then visualize yourself leaving the room and returning to your sacred space, feeling confident as you open your eyes.**

• **Stretch and perform a grounding technique.**

Record your impressions in your Book of Enchantment.

VARIATION

You may enhance the success of this exercise by using an actual chalkboard or a white board with markers or something you can write a question or problem on and then erase very easily.

When you create your sacred space, actually write the question out. Then close your eyes and visualize the scene described above. When you leave your sacred space and open your eyes, immediately erase the problem. This sends a message of confidence and trust that you will get the answer you are seeking. You know the problem will be solved just like erasing it from a chalkboard.

God gives
every bird its food,
but
He doesn't throw
it in the nest.

J.G. Holland

Suggestions for Parents

➤ **One of the best ways for adults to bring out the most creative and psychic abilities in young people is through acceptance.**

Don't belittle or exaggerate the young person's experiences or abilities. Acknowledge their interest. Share and explore with them with an open mind. This not only keeps the doors open but also develops a healthier psychological outlook in the young person.

➤ **Never force a young person to participate in any psychic activities, especially things like esp tests.**

Whatever activities you do with the young persons in your life, make it all seem like a fascinating game. In this way, they are more likely to want to play and explore and feel safe doing so.

➤ **Never turn a young person in your life into a carnival act for family and neighbors.**

Nothing could be more damaging to young people. It is difficult enough for professional psychics to deal with the public and many have great difficulty when they first become public with their abilities.

Be proud of a young person's skills and abilities, but be careful to avoid being one of those parents who try to take control of their young person's accomplishments or live through them.

Sincere praise, encouragement, and acceptance is the best way to bring out anyone's most creative and beneficial qualities. It is particularly essential to young people who are exploring new worlds.

Appendix

Questions
from Kids

I get a tremendous amount of mail every year, and in the past seven to eight years, the amount of mail from young people has increased amazingly. From a third to a half of all the letters I receive are now from young people who are having psychic experiences and would like help in understanding them.

Some of the most common questions I'm asked by these young people about psychic matters are addressed on the following pages.

My friends and family don't understand this stuff. What should I do?

It is difficult enough when other people think your interests are strange, but the hard part is this makes you feel like you don't fit in. Leading a magical life can be difficult at times, especially if you are made to feel like an outsider, but if you continue being the good friend you have always been to those around you, in time they will see that you are not so "strange" after all.

If they are genuinely interested, let them read what you are reading. Treat it like a game. But introduce them to it slowly. Most people do not like to see things change around them. If your friends see you can explore new realms and still be fun and interesting to be with, just as you have always been, in time they will accept the changes in the new you even if they don't believe in the magic you are bringing into your life.

Be careful about trying to prove anything to them through "tests" of your abilities. This will only create doubts and fears in your own mind. Real friends wouldn't put you in a spot like this, trying to turn you into a show-off performer.

Your family might worry they are going to "lose" you, or at least the you they think you are. Be patient with them and talk with them as much as possible, but as with your friends, take it slowly.

Tell them about the things you have learned. If possible, ask your family to play the psychic games and do some of the other activities with you as well. Suggest they read these books so they can come to understand there is nothing in them to fear.

If you are working on getting your family to respect your beliefs, begin by showing them that the things you are discovering do not interfere with your life. Keep your studies and activities up. Let them see that you are becoming more creative and self-assured. Persist, and in time, even if your family and friends do not believe in what you believe, they can still believe and trust in you.

What should I do when people make fun of what I believe?

Sad to say, people do make fun of anything they think isn't normal—which they usually define as anything that isn't just like them. Then there are those who for whatever reason simply do not like us. We all run into these kinds of people whether we are living a magical life or not.

Sometimes, however, you can bring these kinds of problems upon yourselves. You may become so excited about your magical studies you enthusiastically tell anyone and everyone about it. This can invite criticism from those who do not understand. Sometimes it's best to simply go quietly about what you are studying. Be truthful if people ask, but be low key about it all.

When you start awakening your psychic power and your magical selves, some people will respond strongly—and negatively—to you. On some psychic level they recognize your awakening power and strength. They don't understand or even realize your new power has triggered a response in them. But they still feel somehow threatened and they respond defensively. If this happens, stay calm, ignore it as much as possible, and avoid the person. Just continue your magical and psychic work. In time your energy will become strong enough that it will repel these people's negativity, sending it back to them, and they become their own worst enemies.

I touched a friend and got impressions. Should I tell her?

It is sometimes difficult to decide how much to tell. Many people don't like to know things, especially if they are not good things. Sometimes you can get an idea through conversation with your friend about whether the person will accept what you have to say. Sometimes it is good to just ask, "If I knew something, would you want me to tell you?" Consider whether revealing your impressions might hurt the person, especially if they turn out to be incorrect. Remember, interpreting impressions correctly is very tricky.

A psychic has great responsibility. It is very easy to hurt someone with misinformation. Once words are spoken, they can never be taken back. If you are at all unsure, I would recommend just remaining silent until you are completely confident about what your impressions mean, and even then, tell your friend only if he or she truly wants to know.

I feel auras but I do not see them. Can I learn to see them?

Feeling auras is a wonderful thing. You can sense when someone makes you uncomfortable. You know whether or not you like and don't like a person as soon as you meet them. You can even learn to make others feel your aura so that when you walk into a room, everyone notices.

In an earlier book of mine, *How to See and Read the Aura,* I provided exercises that stimulate and strengthen the rods in your eyes, which help your eyes to perceive more light. This, in turn, helps in sensing the aura. Seeing the aura, however, is the easy part. Interpreting what you see is very difficult.

The fact that you can feel auras is wonderful and means you already are sensitive to these energies. Work on developing psychic touch, and in time the other psychic senses, including vision, will awaken.

Is reading tarot cards a sin or demonic?

Unfortunately, people ask me this question far more than I would like. When adults don't understand something, they like to put a label on it. Often that label is based on their own fears.

Psychic ability is natural for all of us. The tarot is simply a tool to help us tap into this natural ability and bring it out. But because the pictures seem strange and are not understood by people who haven't studied them, people are often uncomfortable around tarot cards and assume there is something wrong with them.

Some of the tarot decks do have strange and somewhat bizarre images and artwork, but there are many different tarot decks available, some with very beautiful and comforting images. My *Animal-Wise Tarot*, for example, uses only real animal photographs, and many people can relate to animals without becoming incomfortable. There are also tarot decks of angels, faeries, and other less frightening images. When you start to work with the tarot, start with some of these decks.

After you have found the tarot deck you like, you might try discussing it with whoever has labeled the tarot evil or sinful. Most people resist change of any kind, but especially change in their beliefs, including religious ones. They may well be like the Gorgon in Volume I whose very gaze freezes us, as if they can prevent us from changing by turning us into stone. When you meet Gorgons and you have offered to help them understand, you may simply have to persist, as quietly as possible, with your own beliefs. Living your own beliefs successfully may encourage these people to open to new possibilities and change their minds.

A psychic told me that my troubles at school
and with my friends are because someone
who was jealous of me was using psychic power
and witchcraft against me. What should I do?

Schools are miniature little worlds and you experience in them the same kinds of things that adults experience in the outside world. This includes dealing with people who are jealous.

It is possible the psychic was right about the jealousy, but usually when psychics tell people something like this, they often follow it up with an invitation to help you—usually for a fee. If efforts were being made through witchcraft or psychic projections to create trouble around you, this report by this psychic seems to highly exaggerate their effects. In general, young people do not have the skills or knowledge necessary to do this kind of thing effectively at all.

Most of the adults in this field who make claims like this are also lacking in knowledge and skills. To be quite truthful, it is far easier to stir up things simply by gossiping than it is by doing real spellwork.

My suggestion would be to ignore anything this psychic told you. Learn to work with your own psychic power and trust in your own perceptions. Don't buy into rumors of psychic intrigue. It can awaken fear and block your own psychic powers.

If we keep ourselves balanced and healthy, if we focus on what we are doing rather than what others are doing, we find that most troubles seem to disappear. Learning to keep ourselves balanced with everything that goes on around us is part of our life's lesson.

My sister had a dream of my father visiting her after he died. Why didn't he visit me? Didn't he really like me?

Yes, your father liked you. Just because he showed up in your sister's dreams and not yours doesn't mean he didn't love you or that he loved your sister more. When most people die, it is difficult for them to communicate with the living, so they often choose the person who's easiest to reach. Most of the time the message is really for the entire family.

A while back a friend of mine died in a way that raised a lot of questions. I had a dream in which she came to visit me. She talked to me about what had happened and asked me to call her mother and her best friend and tell them she loved them and knows how much they loved her.

When I spoke to her mother, she was thrilled because there were so many things she had wanted to say and didn't get a chance to. She was comforted to know that someone had heard from her daughter and that all was well. I am sure my friend came to me to pass on the message because I would be able to do it.

The funeral and other activities around a person's death are very stressful. They disrupt sleep and may make our perceptions a bit off. Even though it is likely your father went to your sister because she was the easiest to speak through at the time, if you stay open to communications, messages will eventually come to you and through you as well. And you will have no doubts about the love of your father.

Glossary

aura   the energy field that surrounds all matter; around humans it is the electro-magnetic field

belief   a pattern of thougts that shape our behavior and life; confidence in the existence of something not readily seen or perceived; to know something truly exists, often without proof

clairaudience (clear hearing)   the hearing of spirits or voices that reveal information; usually refers to psychic perceptions through the sense of hearing, either an inner voice in one's own mind or a disembodied voice from someone in spirit form

clairvoyance (clear seeing)   the seeing of things, events, and people, including spirit; it can also refer to seeing the future or the past; usually a catchall word for psychic perceptions

objective clairvoyance: the ability to see images and have perceptions outwardly with the physical eyes; *subjective clairvoyance*: the ability to see images with the mind

clairsentience (clear feeling)   the ability to sense or feel things, events, and people, including spirits. It is often used to describe when someone has a "psychic feeling or hunch" (See psy-chometry.)

divination   ability to divine or know the future; information coming to us from a divine source

empathy	a heightened sense of psychic and physical feeling
esp	extra-sensory perception; psychic and intuitive perceptions; knowing things beyond what is usually known by the five senses of sight, taste, touch, smell, and hearing
glamour	enchantment that attracts and influences
ground	to be balanced; eliminating "spacey" or "out-of- sorts" type of feelings; to regroup and gather one's senses about one's self
imagination	the image-making faculty of the mind; it is used in all psychic and creative activities, including the receiving and sending of thoughts
intuition	psychic perceptions; the inner knowing and feeling
karma	to do; often thought of as cause and effect, but it is more what results from our life experiences; by choices we make and actions we take, certain events unfold for us
magic	wisdom; the ability to make life work more effectively by applying natural and spiritual laws, wisdom and natural abilities such as clairvoyance and psychism

Glossary

manifest   to make happen; to bring into being; to help bring about

occult   things that are hidden; usually associated with psychic mysteries

psychic   the ability to tap one's intuition or use ESP, clairvoyance, or mental telepathy to know things about oneself, other people, places, or events, including perceptions of the spirit world

psychometry   the ability to pick up impressions from objects, places, and people through touch and a heightened sense of feeling

shapeshifting   the ability to transform; to change one's shape, energy, and form

supernatural   beyond things that are natural; in reality, things of the supernatural are things just misunderstood at this time—psychic phenomena were once considered supernatural but are no longer as they become recognized as natural to all people

telepathy   ability to send and receive physical, mental, or emotional messages

Andrews, Ted. *How to Develop and Use Psychic Touch*. St. Paul, MN; Llewellyn Publications,1994.

> Explores in simple language how to do more with psychic touch, including how to tune to objects, places, and people.

Andrews, Ted. *How to Meet and Work with Spirit Guides*. St. Paul, MN; Llewellyn Publications, 1992.

> A simple and practical guide to the entire realm of spirits, including information on working with angels, fairies, and animal totems.

Gawain, Shakti. *Creative Visualization*. New York: Bantam, 1982.

> Wonderful guide to techniques and applications of creative visualization and manifestation. It is good for beginners and a refreshing reminder for everyone of the power of visualization.

Krieger, Dolores. *Therapeutic Touch*. Englewood Cliffs, NJ: Prentice-Hall, 1979.

> Terrific book on using the hands to touch and heal. It may be a bit scientific for some young people, but the exercises are easy to follow and give excellent results. It will help you to sense auras and use healing touch.

Linn, Denise. *Sacred Space*. New York: Ballantine Books, 1996.

> A very practical guide filled with many techniques and tools for creating and strengthening your own sacred space.

INDEX

Young Person's School of Magic and Mystery
VOLUME III

Dreamtime Magic

by

Pagyn Alexander

Hardbound

224 pages

$18.95 USA

ISBN 1-888767-38-3

In *Dreamtime Magic* you will learn how to understand and work with your dreams:

- to improve dream recall,

- to interpret dreams,

- to control your dreams.

- to create dream doorways, and

- to fight the monsters under your bed.

You will also learn to use dreams for creative expression, for self-healing, and for personal growth.

Young Person's School of Magic & Mystery
VOLUME IV

Star Magic

by

Page Bryant

Hardbound

256 pages

$18.95 USA

ISBN 1-888767-
44-8

Uncover the mystery and magic of the heavens! In *Star Magic*, you will learn how:

- to become a star shaman,
- to read the night sky,
- to create a star body,
- to meet the star people,
- to collect and use sacred star objects,
- to make a sacred star bundle,
- to awaken the magic of the sun and moon, and
- to become a starwalker.

Also by
Ted Andrews

Psychic Protection

**Develop the
Tools for
Protection and Balance!**

At a time when so much information is available and so many present themselves as experts, a down-to-earth manual of psychic principles and common-sense practices has never been so needed. From one of today's most experienced and best teachers in the psychic and holistic fields comes a handbook for psychic self-defense that everyone can use.

This book provides practical scientific and spiritual tools for protecting our environment, our lives, and ourselves and will make the spiritual quest safer, more creative, and more fulfilling.

⭐Winner of
Visionary Award* for
best spirituality book!

⭐Runner-Up
1999 Visionary Award* for
best self-help book!

358 pages   **$12.95 USA**

ISBN 1-888767-30-8

Available from
Dragonhawk Publishing
P.O. Box 1316
Jackson, TN 38302-1316

---

*   Visionary Awards presented by the Coalition of Visionary Retailers at the 1999 International New Age Trade Show.

Also by Ted Andrews

The Animal-Wise Tarot

The Animal-Wise Tarot contains 78 full-color cards of actual animal photographs and a 248-page soft-cover text.

$34.95 USA

ISBN 1-888767-35-9

Available from
Dragonhawk Publishing
P.O. Box 1316
Jackson, TN 38302-1316

⭐ Runner-Up Visionary Award* for best spirituality book!

Discover the Language of Animals!

All traditions taught the significance of Nature—particularly of the animals crossing our paths, whether we are awake or dreaming. Use The Animal-Wise Tarot to develop your intuition, strengthen your connection to the animal world, and to find the answers to your most puzzling questions in life.

Whether an experienced tarot enthusiast, a shamanic practitioner, or a novice to psychic exploration, this tarot's clarity and ease of use will be a refreshing surprise. Anyone can use this tarot effectively from the moment it is opened and you will find yourself becoming truly animal-wise!

* Visionary Awards presented by the Coalition of Visionary Retailers at the 1999 International New Age Trade Show.

About the Author

Ted Andrews is an internationally recognized author, storyteller, teacher, and mystic. A leader in the human potential, psychic, and metaphysical fields, he has written over 24 books which have been translated into many different languages.

Ted has been involved in the serious study of the esoteric and occult for more than 30 years, and he brings to the field a very extensive formal and informal education. A former public school teacher and counselor, he worked mostly with disadvantaged inner city youth. His innovative reading programs received both local and state recognition.

Ted also has many years of hands-on experience with wildlife rehabilitation, possessing state and federal permits to work with birds of prey. He has served as a trail guide and naturalist for children of all ages. He conducts animal education, storytelling programs, and metaphysical seminars throughout the U.S and Europe.

Called a true Renaissance man, Ted is schooled in music, hypnotherapy, accupressure, and other healing modalities. He has composed, performed, and produced the music for ten audiocassettes and he is a continuing student of ballet and kung fu.